PUTTING T

In search of a Liberal Jewish theology

Pete Tobias
January 2020

Also by Pete Tobias

This book is dedicated to the members of
the Tuesday morning Adult Education class
at The Liberal Synagogue Elstree, for whom
each chapter was written on a Monday, and
inflicted on them the following morning.

And to Rabbi David Goldberg *z'l*
who sadly never got to read it but
would, I hope, have approved.

I have made every effort to acknowledge
any external sources. I apologise if I have
failed to do this successfully.

ISBN 978-0-244-55160-5

George the Monkey Productions 2020

CONTENTS

INTRODUCTION:

THE MISSING 'O'[1]

G dash D. That's who I was told I had to believe in. Of course you could actually say the word God. But you couldn't write it down. So if you wrote it anywhere – on a chalkboard, on a piece of paper – even if you wanted to graffiti it on a wall somewhere – you had to miss out the middle letter. So instead of the middle letter, you put a dash. G dash D.

Who or what was this G dash D, this person, this being that might just as easily be Gad or Gid, Ged or Gud – even Gyd, at a pinch – instead of the name we weren't supposed to write down?

One of Judaism's finest skills has been the extraordinary lengths it has gone to in order not to say the name of its deity. In the Torah, the name is made up of four Hebrew letters *yud, hei, vav* and *hey*.[2] To the bafflement and

---

[1] The first part of this book (and much of the second) is specifically about the development of the Jewish G-d and the religion that was - constructed around that ancient concept. Although much of it is very specific to Judaism, I believe that there are certain truths that can, without too much difficulty, be transferred to other religions and their relationship with their scriptures.
[2] See page 108

consternation of many a *bar-* or *bat-mitzvah* student, the pronunciation of this combination of letters is *Adonai* – translated as 'My Lord'[3] but is certainly not what those letters say. Then, after an ingenious combination of the four letters YHWH[4] and the vowels of *Adonai,* you end up with *Y'hovah* – another name that isn't really the name of G–d: Jehovah. And there are many, many more: *Ha-Shem* (the Name), *Ha-Kadosh Baruch Hu* (the Holy One, blessed be He[5]) being among the more common.

It would appear that, in the earliest days of Israel's contact with its deity, the pronunciation of that deity's name brought fear and terror. No wonder the commandment not to take G–d's name in vain was right up there at number three. Terrible things would happen if the wrong person said the unpronounceable name at the wrong time or in the wrong place.

––––––––––––––––

[3] Actually *Adonai* is plural, meaning 'my Lords', but that's rather problematic for a religion that prides itself on having one G–d. It probably emanates from the Hebrew word *elohim*, another word used for the Israelite God that is also plural. This derives from the fact that the Israelite deity was established to contain all the gods worshipped by other nations. Incidentally, traditional Jews may even write 'L–rd' and read *Adonai* as *Adoshem,* such is the obsession with not pronouncing or writing the Divine Name

[4] The '*vav*' is represented in Roman letters as a 'W' as the idea was initiated by German scholars in the 19th Century.

[5] A G–d is, almost inevitably, bound to be male, I'm afraid, as the concept of a god in ancient times was mainly as a battle mascot or a warrior.

And so began the relationship between the Israelite people, later to become the Jews, and their God (yes, I put the 'o' in, because I believe it was there at the start!). It was a relationship based on fear, on an obsession with trying (too) hard not to do the wrong thing. It was an exercise that turned God into G–d, as human beings created and became obsessed with religion and ritual. In so doing, I believe, they removed the very heart of the God that religion and ritual purported to be seeking.

PART ONE of this book looks at how the 'o' was removed from God: how religion developed, how the Torah was written and compiled and how its very essence was lost when it was claimed that God had written it. God doesn't write books. Human beings write books. Some of them are good and profound; others are clumsy, perhaps well meaning but ultimately misguided. The Torah contains all these elements. I believe that the way to put the 'o' back into the G–d created by the incorrect belief about the authorship of the Torah is to re-examine it. The challenge is to separate that which is clearly human and flawed from that which is inspired by the divine. This is the role and responsibility of liberal-thinking Jews: Jews who love and respect their Jewish heritage but are troubled, just as were the biblical prophets before them, by the emphasis on ritual correctness at the expense of ethical behaviour. A Liberal reading of the Torah and the Jewish experience that surrounds its development and transmission is essential if we wish to put the heart back into G–d.

Except in certain cases, I have referred to the deity as G–d throughout Part One. This is mostly to serve as an irritant and to represent the extent to which, in my opinion, our current views on and attitudes towards the divine are misguided and misdirected. Our current efforts to find God in our world through the practice of religion are doomed to fail because of the fact that we have removed God's heart from the venture we call religion.

PART TWO will then look at how we might reclaim the reverence and awe, the respect and appreciation that our ancestors had for their world. These are qualities that we seem to have lost. I once said that God wishes only for human beings to grow, and to achieve their potential. I would say that God actually *is* our human potential.[6] And, as I hope to show, the way to rediscover our ancestors' appreciation of and gratitude for their world is to insert a second 'o': put an 'o' in God – turn God, our human potential, into Good. We must work to make our contribution the Godliness and 'Goodliness' of a world where we seek to be a little more caring, a little kinder. We should each seek to bring a little goodness into our lives and the lives of those around us. It's really not very complicated...

'For this commandment that I am commanding you today is not too difficult for you, nor is it too remote.

---

[6] Tobias, P. 'Why Am I Here, p.93

It is not in heaven that you might say 'Who will go up to heaven for us to fetch it for us and make it known to us that we might understand it?' Nor is it across the sea that you might say 'Who will go across the sea for us to fetch it for us and make it known to us that we might understand it?' No. This thing is very close to you – on your lips and in your hearts that you might do it.'

Deuteronomy 30:11-13

Rabbi Pete Tobias
Camarillo, California. January 2020

PART ONE

PUTTING THE 'O' IN G–D

13

1 THE G–D YOU DON'T BELIEVE IN

Whenever I find myself in conversation with anyone who gives me a patronising look and proudly asserts that they don't believe in G–d, I find myself wanting to ask this question: 'So please can you tell me about the G–d you don't believe in?'

If they were Professor Richard Dawkins (and yes, I've had the conversation with him too[7]) they might list some of the 16 adjectives he uses in his book 'The God Delusion'[8] to describe the deity he describes as a 'control freak,' an 'ethnic cleanser' and 'a bully'. The attributes assigned to the 'Old Testament G–d' include misogynistic, homophobic and genocidal.

That's also the kind of G–d that a vast majority of people don't believe in. It's a definition of G–d that sits comfortably alongside the image of the old man with the long beard sitting on a cloud looking down on the people below, watching for signs of bad behaviour and hurls lightning bolts at will.

---

[7] I was invited to a showing of the film *The Unbelievers* that was followed by a Q&A session with Richard Dawkins and Lawrence Krauss. There was a polite but futile conversation in which I said that I agreed with Prof Dawkins' attitude to the God of the Old Testament and he replied that was because I was 'a nice young man.'

[8] Dawkins R., 'The God Delusion', p.37

Nevertheless, it seems that an alarming number of people do believe in this G–d. Such people are the worthy targets of Dawkins' ire: they give religion and God a bad name, inviting ridicule and criticism. Another story that he quotes relates to the Asian tsunami of Boxing Day 2004. More than a quarter of a million people died in an event that affected the coastlines of several countries. Dawkins speaks of an Asian leader who believed that the event was a consequence of human sin[9]. This opinion was borne out in a documentary in 2009 in which three survivors from different affected countries were interviewed. One was Muslim, one Christian and one Hindu. Against a background of devastated coastal villages that had once been their homes, each affirmed the belief, from within their own religious tradition, that the event five years earlier had been a punishment from their G–d.

Poor G–d. Being held responsible for all that destruction. All those innocent lives, all the victims of countless natural disasters through the centuries. The very fact that G–d can allow such suffering is, for so many, confirmation of His non-existence. So the answer to my initial question, the heading of this chapter asking for a description or definition of the G–d you don't believe in is becoming clear. You don't believe in the G–d who either punishes human beings randomly, or who simply fails to intervene when the lives of innocents are in danger. What rational person could possibly believe in such a G–d?

---

[9] *Ibid.* p. 238

One last example of someone who does. Rabbi Harold Kushner, in his book 'When Bad Things Happen to Good People'[10], tells how as a young rabbi, he was required to visit the home of a family whose young child had been killed in a road traffic accident. Nervously he knocks on the door, wondering how he, as a rabbi, can explain the place of G–d in this tragedy. The boy's grieving father opens the door, and before he even crosses the threshold, Kushner has been told 'Don't worry, rabbi. We know why this happened. It's because we didn't go to synagogue last Yom Kippur, isn't it?'[11]

Of course it isn't. That's not why the child died. Any more than the deaths of 19 Israeli schoolchildren who, in 1985, were killed when their bus became trapped on a level crossing and was struck by a train[12] could be blamed on violations of the Sabbath laws in their home town of Petach Tikvah and faulty *mezuzot*[13] at their school.

---

[10] Kushner H., 'When Bad Things Happen to Good People', Pan Books, 1981.

[11] *Ibid.* It appears that in my memory I have conflated two different episodes described in the book. The response of the father in the episode I describe relates to the sudden death of his 19 year-old daughter (p.5-6 of his book); the (non-Jewish) boy killed in the road traffic accident is absurdly eulogised by his family's clergyman (p.8). I have been using my example for so long that I hope Harold Kushner will forgive me!

[12] The Ha-Bonim disaster of June 11 1985.

[13] *Mezuzot* (plural; singular *mezuzah*) - the small case containing parchment with the biblical text of the *Sh'ma* (Deuteronomy 6:4-9; 11:13-21; Numbers 15:37-41) found on the doorposts of the vast

These and countless other disasters or accidents took place as a result of human error and basic physics. If a car hits a small boy, or a train travelling at 60 mph hits a stationary school bus, the consequences are inevitable. And unless you believe in a G–d who is watching over everything and who can alter nature – or not – whenever He feels like it, you can't really expect G–d to prevent what must surely follow. But if you don't believe in such a G–d, then you can comfortably point to such incidents as further evidence for your non-belief. And there you have the perfect definition of the G–d that the majority of people appear not to believe in.

This – quite literally – unbelievable G–d is the one who features in the Torah, the Hebrew Bible and the Jewish prayerbook. In addition to a whole range of improbable actions and behaviour, He supports the falling, He heals the sick, He even 'sets the stars in their courses in the sky'.[14] If you want a comprehensive definition of a G–d who is almost impossible to believe in, look no further than these Jewish books. But if you want justification for not believing in G–d, simply apply 21st century logic and rationale to the vast majority of prayers uttered in a synagogue – yes, even the Liberal ones – and your case is proven. Here is a G–d you cannot possibly believe in. But I don't believe in that G–d either. So if you say you 'don't

---

majority of Jewish homes. This outrageous 'explanation' for this tragic accident was made by Yitzchak Peretz, a Member of the Knesset (Israeli Parliament) who represented the Shas (Orthodox religious) party.
[14] e.g. 'Siddur Lev Chadash' Liberal Judaism, 1993 p.93

believe in G–d', we actually have more in common than you might think.

Many, many years ago an aunt sent me a birthday card which told this interesting story. I'm pretty sure it was long before I began my journey to becoming a rabbi, so I don't think she was trying to tell me anything. Inadvertently, however, she most certainly did.

There were four different cartoon images on the front of the card. The first three depicted a man set against the background of rising water caused by incessant rainfall. In the first, with only a few inches of water on the ground, a fire engine drove up his street. The firemen called to the man, who was looking out of his living room window, telling him to get on their truck. The second picture showed the man on the first floor of his house, talking to some men in a lifeboat, which had sailed up to his house on water that was now several feet deep. He was on the roof in the third picture, a rope ladder that had been lowered from a helicopter dangling close to him as the water threatened to cover his entire house. In each of the pictures the man was being implored to leave his home and travel to safety with those who were trying to rescue him. To each of them he gave the same reply. 'I believe that G–d will save me,' he said as he declined their offers of help.

The fourth picture, at the bottom of the front of the card, showed the man in what was presumably heaven. He was standing before an enthroned man (bearded, obviously) surrounded by angels. The drowned man is protesting to the G–d that he believed in. 'I have always trusted in You!' he cries. 'Why did You let me drown?'

Opening up the card, we find this bearded man-G–d's response. 'I sent you a fire engine, a lifeboat and a helicopter,' says G–d, surrounded by angels. 'What else did you want me to do?' Then it says 'Happy Birthday Peter from Auntie Trudy and Uncle Jack xx' but that's not really the point of the story.

That story came to mind a few years ago when a group of 33 miners in Chile were trapped 2,300 feet below ground for 69 days. In addition to the various mining experts and engineers who gathered on the Chilean hillside to rescue them were various religious leaders who set up vigil on the miners' behalf. While the experts laboured away drilling escape shafts, the religious leaders presumably prayed on their behalf. When the men were brought to the surface more than two months after they had become trapped, their rescuers quietly cleared away their equipment. The religious leaders each claimed it had been their influence on G–d that had saved the miners. Meanwhile, a couple of days later, a similar disaster in a mine in China caused the deaths of 29 people. Was G–d not there? Does He prefer Chileans to Chinese? Does G–d perform miracles on an alphabetical basis? Or was it because the safety standards in Chinese mines were greatly inferior?

These are not really questions about God. They are questions about what most people imagine G–d to be or wish that G–d was. And because G–d isn't those things, the logical conclusion is that it is not possible to believe in G–d. Well, I don't believe in that G–d either.

What we are dealing with here is G dash D. A divine power who, it is assumed, can order the universe according to the needs of any individual. In this world view, each individual can communicate with the Divine but, in most cases, is unlikely to do so unless something goes wrong in his or her life – at which point G–d gets the blame. My intention is to find a more meaningful, subtle understanding of God – perhaps one that is hinted at by scientist Carl Sagan when he says '...If by "God" one means the set of physical laws that govern the universe, then clearly there is such a God.'[15]

That doesn't sound to me like the G–d you don't believe in, the one with the missing centre. But it's the God I wrestle with, and the one we need to think about more carefully.

---

[15] Quoted in "Scientists & Their Gods" in *U.S. News & World Report* Vol. 111 (1991)

But before we do, I'd like to explore how humankind in general, and my ancient Israelite ancestors in particular, tore the heart out of God and created G–d almost as soon as they had first encountered the Divine.

2 - WHO CREATED G–D?

One of the favourite bits of my rabbinic work is talking to primary school children. I used to be a teacher of 10-11 year-olds and they remain my favourite age group. I left teaching in 1985, just as Sir Keith Joseph introduced the National Curriculum – an exercise, it still seems to me, intended to reduce children to the level of statistics and squeeze the life out of their creativity and potential.

There's a section of the English Religious Education Curriculum requiring children in school Years 2 and 5 to investigate the role of religious leaders. So every April I am inundated with requests to visit schools. I try to manage as many as I can, because I love being able to walk into a classroom, entertain, challenge and laugh with the children, then leave, without having to do any marking or write up any lesson notes explaining what targets I have reached.

And they ask some great questions. Some pretty ordinary ones too ('What's your favourite colour/food?' for example). But things like 'What made you decide to become a rabbi?' or 'Who created G–d?' demonstrate a level of curiosity, naiveté and openness that adults have mostly left behind.

They're difficult questions to answer – mostly because there's not enough time and the other children want to find out how old I am or what football team I support. But if I have enough time, this is roughly what I say to my ten-year-old audience:

'Imagine you were living thousands of years ago. No electricity. No running water. No computers or TV. A 'house' made of mud and straw. When the sun goes down you have no idea whether or not it will come back again. And there is nothing to lighten the darkness except the moon, which has a slightly different shape each night and a sky filled with millions of stars.

'So when the sun comes back you feel relief and you feel gratitude towards whatever makes that happen. But lots of other things come from that sky as well. Sometimes it rains – which is good, because you need water. But sometimes it rains too much and causes floods, which can be a problem. And sometimes it doesn't rain at all, which means that nothing grows and you and your family can die of starvation. Then there are storms – imagine what you would think when you saw lightning and heard thunder for the first time! Something terrible is happening! And earthquakes, and wild animals and diseases that might kill you or those around you – all these things that happen without warning, without explanation. Life is bewildering and terrifying.

'But even in that state of terror and bewilderment, you might start to notice certain patterns. The changing shape of the moon was not random: it had a very distinct sequence that repeated regularly. The sun also followed a pattern: sometimes it was lower in the sky and was only visible for a short period of time; other times it was higher and it rose earlier, set later. And when it was around for longer and went higher in the sky, the climate was much warmer. And so on and so on...

'Gradually someone in your tribe works out that the seasons follow one another in a repeating pattern. Eventually you come up with the earliest calendar, using the phases of the moon and connecting these units of time to the seasons.' But that's a different story, which I have looked at more closely elsewhere.[16]

Because although our ancient ancestors began to find ways to measure the passage of time, they still didn't understand much about how the world actually worked. And there was much in their environment that continued to alarm and frighten them. And although we sophisticated 21st century adults might have difficulty imagining how we might feel in such a world, children understand it pretty quickly. It doesn't take long to get them to come up with the idea of the ancients imagining or believing that there was someone or something somewhere that was

---

[16] See e.g. Tobias, P; *Never Mind the Bullocks* 2009 p.73

controlling these climatic forces that had such an influence on and power over the lives of our ancient ancestors. And then they can make pretty rapid steps in suggesting that trying to communicate with whatever that something or someone was would be a good idea. A combination of trial and error, guesswork, common sense and coincidence would lead to the establishment of a series of rituals. Those who practiced them believed they could influence that invisible power that controlled those natural forces. For example, if rain happened to fall after a particular dance or chant, that same dance or chant would be employed every time rain was needed. If it subsequently failed to produce the required outcome, it would be assumed that it had been performed incorrectly, so it would be repeated or altered slightly until it succeeded.

Whatever were the rituals that 'worked', and whoever were the people entrusted to perform them on the people's behalf, would become the practices, beliefs and leaders of a particular tribal group. But those practices and beliefs have nothing to do with God. This is religion. And it's pretty clear that God and religion are two very different things. People created religion – and the more 'successful' a series of practices were seen to be and, more specifically, the more powerful were the priestly group that oversaw and managed them, the more entrenched these religious beliefs would become in the culture of individual tribal groups.

So early human beings assumed the existence of a G–d because of the need for an explanation of why mysterious and unpredictable events occurred. Not so different from the victims of the Asian tsunami or the young child killed in the road traffic accident in chapter one.[17] The G–d we don't believe in. Our ancestors did, however. It helped them to make sense of seemingly random, often destructive events.

So arose the rather trivial observation that human beings created G–d. It refers to the G–d that we don't believe in. It's a view of G–d that emerged when humanity was in its infancy. As such, it's bound to be a pretty infantile concept. According to a scale of the development of faith constructed in the 1980s by psychologist James Fowler,[18] there are six stages of spiritual development towards which human beings should aspire. He calls the first stage 'intuitive-projective' – a pre-school stage in which fantasy and reality are often mixed and basic ideas about G–d are picked up from parents and/or society. That sounds like a good description of the concepts that were emerging in early human society.

The second stage is 'mythic-literal', where children of early school age learn and generally accept stories told them by their faith community. In terms of human development,

---

[17] See page 16f

[18] Fowler, James W. *Stages of Faith*, Harper & Row, 1981. See Appendix, p.145-6

this is the manner in which the earliest forms of religion were manifested and transmitted. Isolated from other external influences, any belief system could easily sustain itself. Those who adhered to it in a tribal group would have no need to change their faith or their understanding of the world. Fowler suggests that some people in the world today exist within such self-contained systems, with a very limited, literal understanding of their faith that cannot countenance the existence of alternatives.

Such understandings of G–d would hold true until these ancient tribal groups encountered other tribes with different beliefs. Our ancestors with their childlike views will have struggled to comprehend the existence of other belief systems. In Fowler's terms this would be stage three, which he calls: 'synthetic-conventional'. It's a 'teenage' stage where, after encounters with other groups, there is a need to come to terms with the existence of different systems. They are acknowledged, but only in a token way: people's fundamental beliefs and worldview are still shaped by the beliefs they have learned. Individuals or groups that represent those beliefs are still regarded as having authority and authenticity. Fowler suggests that this is the stage in which many people remain: awareness of an all-encompassing system of belief that is nevertheless rooted in their own belief system.

The higher stages of Fowler's development scale for individuals and its connection with human faith development will be encountered later.[19] All that needs to be acknowledged now is that individuals and the groups they have cultivated remain for the most part in a very underdeveloped state. The fourth of Fowler's stages is effectively a rejection of the belief system with which one has grown up. In a time when organised religion is being rejected – and with it any belief in G–d – this would appear to be where a significant number of people now are. What is needed, I believe, is a more grown-up understanding of God. But I'd still like to explore further how human beings changed God to G–d, thus bringing about this situation.

---

[19] See chapter 12

3 - DOES G–D LISTEN TO PRAYERS?

There are many stages on the journey to develop a grown-up approach to God. One of those must surely be the manner in which we removed the 'o' from God – effectively removing God's heart – and thereby ensnared God in the straitjacket of religion. It comes, I think, from the flawed idea that this invisible power beyond the skies listens to and can be influenced by things we do and words we utter to or at Him.

One of my favourite stories about prayer goes like this. There's a period of silent meditation at the end of the prayer known as the *Amidah*.[20] It's traditionally a time which some people use as an opportunity to make requests of G–d.

One Shabbat morning, Mrs Cohen is sitting at the back of the synagogue. During the silence she whispers a request to G–d. 'Please, G–d, let me win the lottery.' The following Saturday she is back again. During the silence, she whispers 'I asked you last week. Maybe you didn't hear. Please can I win the lottery?' In the following weeks she returns again and again and repeats her request with increasing volume and anger. Eventually when the congregation reaches its

---

[20] The central prayer of Jewish tradition, introduced by the Rabbis 2,000 years ago as a substitute for animal sacrifice.

moment of silent prayer, Mrs Cohen stands up, shakes her fist at the heavens and cries out 'Dear G–d! How many times do I have to ask you? PLEASE LET ME WIN THE LOTTERY!'

And G–d, watching from above, takes a moment off from ordering the universe and calls down: 'Please Mrs Cohen. Do me a favour and meet me halfway. Buy a lottery ticket.'

I think there's an idea that hides inside this story: what actually is the nature of the lottery ticket; what is it that one should buy into in order for prayer to succeed? But before considering that, let us dwell briefly on the absurdity of praying to G–d to fulfil a particular wish or desire. It could be something as trivial as winning the lottery (with or without a ticket), or for one's team to win a football match. Or it could be a life-saving moment like requesting the safe rescue of young boys trapped in a cave in Thailand, or the recovery of someone dangerously or terminally ill.

Any such prayers that make requests of G–d are nonsensical. They are ridiculous demands, directed at the G–d we don't believe in. Why would G–d deliberately select one individual to win a lottery prize just because they prayed (and the other purchasers of tickets didn't pray?) or show preference to one set of football players and their supporters over another? More troubling is the request for G–d to intervene and save life. If the person or persons on whose behalf one is praying survive, the chances are that will be down to the expertise of the rescuers or the skills of a surgical team. And if they don't survive, then what? G–d didn't care for the victims? Or didn't listen to the person who was praying – maybe because they didn't go to synagogue last Yom Kippur? Making ridiculous or impossible requests to G–d demeans the person making them and certainly demeans God.

If an individual finds the kind of prayer that asks G–d for things helpful, perhaps they ought to think more carefully about what they are requesting. Obviously praying for a lottery or sporting win deserves no further comment. But in the case of people in danger, prayers asking that they have the fortitude to deal with their predicament and wishing success to those seeking to save them or reduce their suffering at least have an air of possibility. Nevertheless, it must be said that the purpose and effect of such prayers is probably more for the benefit of the person uttering them than with any real expectation that their prayers will be answered. In such situations, the sense of comfort that such words of prayer can bring to the pray-er, the person searching for hope, consolation or support. For such an individual, prayers do not need to make intellectual sense. Nor do they require or even expect a response from some mystical source. Calling to mind the memory or the need of a loved one in the presence of others with, perhaps, similar yearnings, might offer comfort in a way that cannot be rationally explained.

If we look back to earliest times once more, this aspect of the nature and purpose of prayer becomes clearer. In the naïve and childlike view of our ancient ancestors, there was a need for visual representation of their efforts to communicate with whatever power they believed controlled their lives. To their eyes, the majority of its manifestations emanated from the sky in the form of various weather conditions. So it made sense to direct their requests and their gratitude, their apologies and their praise upwards, towards that sky. They also wanted a visual representation of their yearnings ascending and being received by whatever they believed dwelt there. So began the practice of sacrifice: the offerings to this invisible power being placed on a special table (altar) and ignited. The smoke rises to the heavens and disappears as it climbs higher – creating the impression that it has been accepted on high.

Although we can barely appreciate it now, to those watching and participating in such efforts to communicate with what was perceived as the Almighty, this must have seemed a truly awesome event. And with the passage of time it became increasingly sophisticated, as the offerings were presented by special individuals wearing exotic costumes, accompanied by chants and music and dance. In Israelite history, this worship eventually became limited to the Temple in Jerusalem[21] and, after its second destruction, was replaced in traditional Judaism with words, rather than sacrifice, yearning for a return to that

---

[21] For more on Israelite history, see chapter 4

34

city. All traditional Jewish prayer was directed eastwards, ostensibly towards Jerusalem (approximately: here in the northern hemisphere when we pray facing east from London, for example, we are actually facing Berlin!) and some of it yearned for or requested a return to Jerusalem to offer sacrifices in a rebuilt Temple.[22]

The physical sacrifice of animals ended with the destruction of the Jerusalem Temple in the year 70 C.E. So prayer was seen as a verbal equivalent of that sacrifice – or rather as a temporary replacement for it. The Rabbis who introduced it at that time almost two thousand years ago, believed that the reconstruction of the Temple and reintroduction of sacrificial worship was imminent. After a few centuries, it became clear that as the Jews were now widely spread across the world in many lands, a return to the land of Israel was highly improbable. A more regulated form of prayer was now required. And so, around a thousand years ago, in the 9th century CE, the structure of Jewish liturgy was formalised, giving us pretty much the same order of service that features in standard synagogue services today.

Without going into the actual detail of these prayers,[23] the fact remains that many of them are largely unchanged since Rabbinic times over 1,000 years previously (and now for almost 2,000 years). With the Roman destruction of the

---

[22] Liberal Judaism has rejected this; see chapter 8
[23] See e.g. p.18

Temple, the notion of animal sacrifice may have been lost (but not completely abandoned). But the idea of saying incredible things about G–d, of bestowing improbable characteristics on G–d and of demanding impossible things of G–d remained and indeed proliferated as rabbis, scholars and poets added their words of wisdom to the ever-increasing volume of Jewish prayer. Orthodox Jewish tradition allowed new things to be added but would not allow anything to be taken away, so services just got longer and longer. The act of praying became cumbersome and wearying for many. To many modern Jews it seemed to lose focus and purpose. The enthusiasm, joy and awe that had once accompanied sacrifice faded and prayer became mundane; even an ordeal.

At this point, a new attitude towards prayer was needed. If it wasn't about talking to G–d, then what was prayer for? Liberal Judaism's approach was to suggest that prayer should be both aesthetically and intellectually pleasing. To that end, progressive synagogues changed the content of many prayers to reflect their new approach to the ancient religion of Judaism.[24] They also reintroduced instrumental music to accompany those prayers, a feature that had been absent since the destruction of the Temple 1,800 years earlier. Initially this was just the organ, but since the late 20th century, many other instruments have also been incorporated in services in Liberal synagogues.

---

[24] see e.g. p.82

In his 1992 'Affirmations of Liberal Judaism', the late Rabbi John Rayner included the following assertion: 'We affirm the paramount need for sincerity in worship: we may not say with our lips what we do not believe in our hearts.'[25] This is patently untrue. Although Liberal Judaism has made significant changes to the words uttered in prayer, many improbable assertions remain. We still refer to G–d in terms that are difficult to believe or identify with, and there are many occasions when focusing on the words of prayers in the Jewish liturgy is an unhelpful and even bewildering exercise.

If there are doubts about the efficacy of prayers that make specific requests of G–d, surely even more questions must be asked about the function of prayer as an intellectual exercise. A rational approach to belief and to prayer must ultimately run aground since there is an element of mystery in the concept of praying that cannot be rationally explained. Prayer may bring comfort and a sense of security to many worshippers; but this cannot be defined in rational terms. And nor should it be.

This is borne out in another story, which I believe was about an elderly relative of one of my fellow rabbinic students. It tells of a Jewish man who was devoted to his heritage and who prayed faithfully, dutifully reciting the ancient words every day. Late in life he suffered a stroke

---

[25] John D Rayner 'The Affirmations of Liberal Judaism', ULPS 1992

that robbed him of the ability to speak. He could not utter a single word in conversation with others. But he was still able to recite his daily prayers with fluency and volume. This indicated that, for this man at least, prayer was an exercise that belonged not to the rational side of his brain, which the stroke had destroyed, but to the emotional side, which was intact. This would suggest that prayer is, perhaps, not concerned with the content or meaning of the words of prayer, but rather with the act of praying.

But in the end, it seems to matter little whether prayer is geared to appeal to either the emotional or the rational side of the human brain. The reality is that, based on ever-diminishing attendance at religious institutions in general, prayer does not work for most people. Of course, it provides comfort for those who have no wish to confront such challenging questions. But their belief system is constructed around the G–d we don't believe in, and it seems fair to say that this relationship doesn't really work for God either. A different approach to God and to prayer and religion is surely needed if human beings are going to be able to develop a more grown-up approach to the divine. But before that, more time is needed to explore how our ancient ancestors found God – and how those who followed took what they had found and ruined it.

4 - WHO WROTE THE TORAH?

During my time as rabbi of Glasgow New (Reform)[26] Synagogue, I once advertised a discussion I was holding at the synagogue. I called it 'Who Wrote the Torah?' It almost caused a riot. Local Orthodox rabbis expressed their outrage but also amusement – what do you expect from these Reform rabbis? They don't even know who wrote the Torah! This, of course, was precisely the response I wanted – and it wasn't the only time I caused a stir north of the border...

For those Orthodox rabbis, and indeed for me when I was learning about my heritage as a child in a United (Orthodox) synagogue, the answer was simple. G–d wrote the Torah. So it wasn't a very challenging question, nor indeed, for those outraged and mystified Glasgow rabbis, the basis for a very long discussion. But by this time I'd been involved in Liberal Judaism for almost twenty years, and a rabbi for half that time, so I had already begun to develop some different, rather radical views about the origins of the Torah.

---

[26] There are 2 progressive movements in the UK – Reform and Liberal. They are both progressive; a general distinction would be to say that Reform Judaism will retain a particular custom unless a good reason can be found to omit or remove it, whereas Liberal Judaism will reject that custom unless a good case can be made for retaining it.

To avoid a full-on history lesson, I'm going to come straight out with it and then work backwards. In my opinion, the Torah was not written by G–d, or dictated by G–d to Moses at the top of a mountain in the middle of a desert. It was compiled over a period of decades, perhaps even centuries. It received its final touches from a group of priests, probably in Jerusalem, in the middle of the 5th century B.C.E.[27] That's about eight centuries after Moses purportedly received it on Mount Sinai. So who wrote it?[28]

Around the year 530 B.C.E. a group of people arrived in what remained of the city of Jerusalem. They were returning from exile in Babylon, which was now under Persian rule. This was a remarkable occurrence. Two generations earlier, their ancestors had been taken from there by Babylonian forces who had besieged the city of Jerusalem before destroying it in the year 586 B.C.E. The Babylonians had perfected the art of dominating and subjugating small kingdoms. Once they had laid siege to and then destroyed the cities of a kingdom or tribal group, they then took its rulers, priests and nobles to Babylon and resettled them there, far from their home. They told their captives that their tribal gods had deserted them, and that the Babylonian gods were superior. This was the accepted theology of the time: your god was only as powerful as his last victory. As soon as you were defeated by a stronger

---

[27] Jewish people do not refer to the years counting down to the year 0 as B.C. (Before Christ). The letters B.C.E. are used – Before the Common Era. The upward count thereafter is known as C.E. – Common Era.
[28] See p.71ff

enemy, your god was defeated also. Add to that the geographical relocation of the key figures of a particular society, and the group lost its identity. Many of the enemies that the Israelites faced in the books of Numbers or Judges, for example, simply disappeared. We hear nothing of the Midianites, the Edomites, the Moabites, the Amalekites and many other –ites[29] beyond the times of King David once he defeats the Jebusites to capture the city of Jerusalem. Their leaders and gods were absorbed into whichever major power annihilated their ancestral home, and the people over whom they once ruled became – probably unknowingly – citizens of a distant empire.

One particular group of –ites are of special interest to us. The Israelites. Again, no history lesson here to explain why, after the death of David's son Solomon, there was a kingdom of Israel and a kingdom of Judah. But the Israelites suffered the same fate as all those other –ites in the year 722 B.C.E. when they fell victim to the might of the Assyrian empire. The Israelite tribes vanished and became the 'ten lost tribes'[30] of popular mythology. According to the legend, Jerusalem, the capital city of the kingdom of Judah, was also besieged, but the Assyrian army retreated after they were affected by a plague. This persuaded the people of Judah of the power of their G–d, the invincibility of Jerusalem and the permanence of the House of David that continued to rule there. Wiser

---

[29] e.g. Canaanites, Amalekites, Hittites etc.

[30] The ten lost tribes of Israel have, according to a variety of myths, improbably reappeared in different places across the globe in the centuries after the destruction of Israel.

Judahite heads recognised that what had happened to the tribes of Israel could – and almost certainly would – happen to Judah also. And they were determined that the beliefs and the traditions and the history of their tribe, enshrined in the city of Jerusalem, should not be lost.

A quick word about Jerusalem. It occupies a central role in Jewish history and tradition. It also features in other religions. In the grand scheme of Ancient Near Eastern history, however, it was a very minor city. David chose it because it was easy to defend. It was perched on a tall hill surrounded by several others, at the heart of the Judean Hills. The major empires of the day were Egypt to the south of what is now Israel and whoever dominated Mesopotamia to the north. There were two main routes, used either for traders or soldiers travelling between these two locations. One was the Way of the Sea: the route that went close to the Mediterranean, through much of the land that once belonged to the defeated kingdom of Israel. The other was the Way of the King, which went to the east of the Judean Hills, through the flat lands of the west bank of the River Jordan, past Jericho. The city of Jerusalem was high up in the hills that lay between those two routes. As such its apparent invincibility owed more to its obscure geographical location and its strategic irrelevance than to any divine protection.

As mentioned, the big players in the region in the first millennium B.C.E. were Egypt and Mesopotamia. The latter was far more volatile, and this area's major ruling power often changed. The Assyrians, who had defeated and dispersed the northern Israelite tribes were themselves vanquished by the Babylonians.[31] The new rulers to the north of Judah quickly asserted their power over their smaller neighbours. One key difference it seems was that the Babylonian emperor, Nebuchadnezzar, was interested in the art, literature and worldview of his captives. This meant that many of the ideas, stories and beliefs of the defeated peoples survived in the cosmopolitan hub that was Babylon, even as those people surrendered their connection to them and became Babylonians. Although the rulers of Judah based in Jerusalem were suspicious of and hostile to anything Babylonian, a group of Judahite scribes found their approach intriguing, and were sympathetic to their way of thinking.

I promised that this wasn't going to be a history lesson, so I won't give you too many more names and dates. But in the thinking of current biblical scholars, two important names are Shaphan and the prophet Jeremiah. It would appear that Shaphan, a senior scribe in the court of Judah, was very impressed with many of the Babylonian advances in a variety of fields. He was convinced that his kingdom of Judah would do well to co-operate with, and learn from, the northern power. Jeremiah shared his views.

---

[31] With the Medes, but Babylon is the power that has a role to play in the story of Judaism.

Eventually, the Babylonians turned their attention to the little city high in the Judean Hills. They approached the rulers of Judah in 597 B.C.E. and were not well received. It became clear to Shaphan, Jeremiah and their followers that Babylon did not like this attitude and that it was only a matter of time before Jerusalem would be attacked, destroyed and its people taken into exile.

So Shaphan, along with other scribes, began the task of collecting together details of as many of the traditions, the legends, the rituals and the practices of the people of Judah as they could find. It is also likely that they had access to other historical and legal material that had been brought to Jerusalem by northern Israelite scribes fleeing from the Assyrians 150 years earlier. They began the work of compiling a detailed history of the kings of Israel and Judah as well as ancient stories and folktales of times long past. Their aim in doing this was to ensure that the people of Judah would not lose their identity. A written record of their past, for them to hear while they were exiled in Babylon, would ensure this.

And that is precisely what happened. When Shaphan's family were taken into exile along with the other Judahites in 597 B.C.E., the Babylonian officials treated them with respect.[32] While the majority of the Judahites were exiled

---

[32] Gedaliah, governor of the Babylonian province of Judah (who was assassinated by Judahites after 586 B.C.E) was Shaphan's grandson. This indicates the well-established position enjoyed by Shaphan's family in the Babylonian court. Details can be found in chapters 29-36 of the book of Jeremiah and in II Kings 22ff.

and in all likelihood forced to work as slaves labouring on Nebuchadnezzar's many building projects, Shaphan, his sons and fellow scribes probably had access to the literature and legal documents of other cultures while they were in Babylon. Many of these were incorporated in their work. What they wrote was a detailed, if somewhat biased, account of the Israelite people in the land of Canaan, which later became Israel and Judah.[33] They also compiled a mythological history of the origins of the world and the Israelite people. This included tales they discovered and adapted in Babylon (the flood, the Tower of Babel) as well as a compilation of popular folktales about Abraham and Jacob (the book of Genesis); a story of slavery in and escape from Egypt, which, among other things, mirrored the people's experiences in Babylon (Exodus 1-14)[34] and many ancient stories of desert experiences and battles (most of Numbers). They also wrote a kind of prequel to their history books, which became the book of Deuteronomy. These books were in all likelihood read and re-read to the exiles of Judah 'by the rivers of Babylon', leaving them in no doubt about who they were and where they came from.

Some seventy years after they had been exiled in Babylon, that empire was overthrown by the Persians. The new rulers gave the exiles of Judah, who still fondly recalled their home, permission to return to it. Only the most

---

[33] The books of Joshua, Judges, Samuel and Kings.

[34] I am intrigued by the possibility that the Exodus story was actually written to reflect the experience of the Judahites in Babylon; that is a subject for another work.

zealous – mainly priests – chose to return, however. The majority preferred comfortable, wealthy Babylon (now ruled by Persia) to a devastated Jerusalem. Those who returned brought with them this scribal work. They edited it, added to it[35] and called it the Torah.[36]

---

[35] Mostly the second half of Exodus and the book of Leviticus plus some 'corrections': see next chapter.

[36] The word 'Torah' comes from a root meaning 'to flow or throw something'. Hebrew suffixes can adapt the meanings of words, so *Morah* or *Moreh* means 'one who does the flowing' – i.e. an archer whose flowing movement directs the arrow or, more abstractly, a teacher who guides a student. *Torah* then becomes the direction in which the arrow is guided, or the instructions from the teacher.

5 - WHOSE IDEA WAS IT TO SAY G–D WROTE THE TORAH?

That's a much better question. To be honest it's not one I've heard very often, at least not as specifically as that. The answer needs a bit more of a history lesson, I'm afraid. But I think it's worthwhile because it might help to explain where traditional Jewish beliefs came from and how, just like the writing of the Torah itself, they owed more to political necessity than divine command.

Let's recap briefly. A group of people returned from Babylon to Jerusalem, the city in which their grandparents or great-grandparents had lived and which had been destroyed by the Babylonians seventy years earlier. These returning Judahites, known in Hebrew as *Y'hudim,* were the first Jews. The Jews didn't leave Egypt, the Jews didn't march round the city of Jericho to make its walls fall down, the Jews didn't watch as David killed Goliath. They were Israelites. Only now, after the return from Babylon, around 530 B.C.E. can we legitimately call them Jews.

There were probably a fair number of people who actually never left what had been the kingdom of Judah. They were the people of the land, the farmers and peasants, who knew little of the affairs of kings and emperors, and probably cared less. But these people were also Jews, as they now dwelt in the Persian province known as Judah. And one day, from the north, came a group of weary travellers wearing unfamiliar clothes, carrying with them many remnants of their time in Babylon. And, most importantly, they brought with them a book, or rather several books: perhaps on parchment scrolls, perhaps on clay tablets. These were the books that had been written by Judah's scribes, the descendants of Shaphan, the followers of Jeremiah, the men who had ensured that this ruined city of Jerusalem would not be forgotten.

According to the biblical books of the time, Ezra and Nehemiah, those who returned to Jerusalem immediately began rebuilding the Temple and subsequently the walls to surround the city. There are stories of various rivalries with different groups, of a wish to ensure that only those of true Judahite stock would be allowed to dwell in this new Jerusalem. Interestingly, the decision of how to do this was to recognise as Judahites only those children who were born to Judahite mothers, since the fathers might be Babylonian. Perhaps this was where the idea of Jewish status passing through the female line began?

Once the Temple had been rebuilt – initially a significantly more modest structure than its predecessor – sacrifice was reintroduced. The priests re-established their authority with the reintroduction of sacrifice and ever more sophisticated ritual to accompany it. These rules were set out in the book of Leviticus, which was written by members of the priesthood. People from the surrounding countryside as well as residents of the gradually rebuilt

Jerusalem gathered before the Temple at festivals, where sacrifice and ritual were carried out by priests. The role of High Priest, purportedly a direct descendant of Aaron[37], was a much-coveted position. In the absence of a king, the High Priest was the leading political figure of Judah as well as its religious head.

After a few years, the book that had been brought back from Babylon was declared complete. This was after the priestly group had made various corrections, amendments and added an entire book emphasising their significance and importance.[38] This was now the Torah – a word that is more often seen as meaning 'teaching'.[39] It comprised the first five books of the Hebrew Bible, from Genesis to Deuteronomy, telling a story that began with the Creation and concluded with the Israelites on the borders of the Promised Land.[40]

Once its contents had been finalised and agreed, there came the task of making copies of this important document. Some of the people whose role was to serve the priests and oversee the worship in the Temple were

---

[37] Brother of Moses – see e.g. Exodus 4:14
[38] The book of Leviticus
[39] See note 36, page 46
[40] The Samaritans; local neighbours of the people of Judah who distrusted and disliked them intensely (and the feeling was mutual), included the book of Joshua in their 'Torah' – extending the story to include settlement in the land of Canaan

given the job of making copies, not just of the Torah, but also of other writings that had been created and compiled in Babylon and after the return. These scribes knew that their work was important as they diligently copied these 'books' onto parchment scrolls. It is highly unlikely, however, that any of them believed for a moment that the words of one particular book had been written or dictated by G–d. They knew their origins. They knew their history. And they understood that the stories and instructions contained in the Torah were a kind of blueprint for the Jerusalem that was being rebuilt and the structure of the society within and around it.

The change of ruling power in Mesopotamia continued with the passing of time. After the Persians came the Greeks; after the Greeks came the Romans, each of whom assumed governance of Judah. Needless to say there was a good deal of political struggle and infighting among the priests and other elements of the populace as they sought to gain favour in the eyes of the different rulers. But it was the arrival of the Romans, around the middle of the first century B.C.E. that brought the greatest challenge, and the severest hardship, to the Jews, the citizens of what was now known as Judea.

There's a well-known anecdote that says wherever there are two Jews there are three opinions. It is meant to characterise the Jewish propensity for disagreement. Throughout Greek times and on into the years of Roman rule, the division between the priests and the scribes grew wider. The priests were effectively the aristocracy of Judea, playing power games with whomever was ruling Jerusalem at any given time. The scribes, on the other hand, busied themselves with the production of copies of the various books that would, before the arrival of the Romans, be established as the 39 books of the Hebrew Bible.[41]

The most important of these books were the first five, the books that made up the Torah. Although they were held in great esteem, the idea of them being written by G–d would still have been far from the minds of those writing them, reading them or hearing them read. They contained important instructions, but these instructions were clearly for the benefit of an ancient biblical society. One particular group of scribes saw their role as being to adapt and develop these instructions for the benefit of the society in which they lived. They would become the Pharisees, taken from the Hebrew root P-R-SH which means to 'interpret'. In opposition to these interpreters of Torah were the Sadducees; the priests, descendants of Zadok (an alternative name for Aaron).

The arrival of the Romans in Judea brought uncertainty and fear[42]. The Jews felt threatened and yearned for the arrival

---

[41] The final decision regarding the contents of the Hebrew Bible was made in the second century B.C.E.. Anything written thereafter (or that the Rabbis disliked) went into the Apocrypha (additional writings).
[42] Usually dated from 63 B.C.E. when Pompey captured Jerusalem.

of someone who would re-establish an independent Jewish kingdom. This person would be the Messiah – a descendant of King David who would drive the Romans away and re-establish independent Jewish rule over Judah. For many, this would mean the end of life as people knew it; an apocalypse that would lead to the establishment of G–d's kingdom on earth. Several groups formed cults anticipating this occurrence. One such group was the Essenes, who established a settlement in the Judean desert. It seems that this group eventually disappeared, as they were reluctant to admit women to their ranks. All that remained were the scrolls they had written (some copies, some originals) which they placed in large earthenware pots. These would be discovered 2,000 years later and become known as the Dead Sea Scrolls.

Military resistance to the Romans was another option. For many years the Jews proved to be perhaps the most difficult opponents to this new Empire with its well-trained well-equipped legions. Unfortunately, but perhaps predictably, there were several Jewish resistance groups, and they mostly expended their military efforts fighting against each other instead of the Romans. When, after the destruction of the city of Jerusalem, these various 'Zealots' fled together to Masada, their days were numbered[43] and it would be almost sixty years before the Jews could muster an army again.[44]

---

[43] The Roman siege of Masada ended in 73 C.E. when the Zealots committed mass suicide.
[44] Shimon Bar Kochba led a rebellion in 132 C.E. Defeated in 135 C.E.

The Roman destruction of Jerusalem in the year 70 C.E. included the burning down of the Temple. This act, which had huge ramifications for the future of the Jewish religion, had one immediate effect: it rendered the priests impotent. The power this group had previously wielded went up in smoke along with the building that had once provided them with their raison d'etre.

The only group left who could offer any hope of a future for the Jews was the Pharisees. They had also become known as Rabbis – teachers – spreading their interpretation of the books of which they were guardians and copiers. In a fraught age of uncertainly and panic, the people of Judea were likely to hold onto anything that offered them hope. The Rabbis, who lived among and were often drawn from the ordinary citizens of Judea, presented these books – particularly the Torah – as offering the best hope for Jewish identity to be retained. When suspicious Judeans asked what was so special about this book, the Rabbis decided the best way to convince the people to believe them was to say that G–d had written it. With the disappearance of the cultic, military and priestly opposition to the Romans, this seemed the only option. So the Torah, a book now declared to have been written by G–d, became the divinely authored basis for the Jewish religion after the Romans finally banished the people of Judea from their home in the second century C.E.

6 - WHAT DOES AN ORTHODOX RABBI DO?
(How the Torah has been read for 2.000 years)

There's an old joke that suggests rabbis are invisible for six days of the week and incomprehensible on the seventh. That tends to be applied to modern-day rabbis (and I can only hope that it doesn't apply to me!) The rabbis I'd like to talk about here have been gone for almost two thousand years. Their effect, however, still lingers. Their work and influence shaped and moulded the religion being practiced in Judea, beginning in Greek times and continuing through Roman times and on into the early centuries of the first millennium. Their influence was so great – and, in many ways, so revolutionary – that they are usually referred to as the Rabbis, with a capital 'R', to distinguish them from the likes of me.

The word 'rabbi' means 'my teacher'. So what were these teachers teaching, and to whom were they teaching it? The Rabbis were the successors of the Pharisees who, in their turn, had emerged from the group of scribes whose role was to make faithful copies of the writings in which were enshrined the national stories, guidelines and identity of the natives and residents of Judea. Indeed these scriptures were well-known further afield as well: there were communities of exiled Judeans (many of whom had never seen Judea) in Babylon and Alexandria who also had access to the work of the scribes, Pharisees and Rabbis.

As explained in the previous chapter, the Rabbis were one of several groups struggling to survive in an era of brutal oppression under the Romans. The violence meted out by the rulers of Judea and the atmosphere of fear they created in that country created a cauldron of uncertainty and fanaticism. The fact that the Rabbis survived while other groups disappeared at different stages of Roman rule was largely due to the fact that they appeared not to offer an existential threat to Judea's rulers. According to a legend, a crucial event occurred during the siege of Jerusalem (66-70 C.E.) One concession apparently permitted by the Romans was for those who died in the siege to be brought out of the city for burial. Yochanan ben Zakkai, the leader of the Rabbinic faction at the time, was allegedly smuggled out alive from Jerusalem by students who claimed that their teacher was dead, inside the coffin they were carrying. Later emerging from his coffin, Yochanan then went to speak to the Roman general in charge of the army: Vespasian. The Rabbi greeted Vespasian as the future Emperor he would soon be, and requested that he and his students be permitted to leave the city to continue their studies elsewhere. Whether it was Yochanan's charm, or Vespasian's confident mood we will never know, but permission was given to the Rabbi to relocate his students to Yavneh, a town in the Galilee.

So it was that the Rabbis' concept of Judaism managed to survive the Roman destruction where most of the others disappeared.[45] Of course, in keeping with the age-old

_____

[45] See previous chapter.

Jewish tradition of two Jews, three opinions, there were different versions of the Rabbinic interpretation – Karaism[46] and Christianity to name two. But it's the work of the Rabbis and, in particular the method they used to give authenticity to their decision making, that was the basis for Judaism as we know it today.

The genius of the Rabbis actually lay in their sheer hubris. In Greek tragedies, hubris meant human beings behaving in an arrogant manner that challenged the gods. What the Rabbis did was, it could be argued, rather similar. Not only did they claim that G–d had written the Torah. They also put forward the idea that G–d had written it in such a way that, several hundred years after G–d had written it, they, the Rabbis, could interpret it. And – here was the hubris – they believed that G–d had anticipated their interpretations when He[47] had written the Torah.

The chutzpah was breathtaking. It is detailed in the opening section of a collection of their best-known writings, *Pirkei Avot*, usually translated as 'Ethics of the Fathers'.[48] The opening statement reads as follows: 'Moses received the Torah from Sinai and transmitted it to Joshua;

---

[46] Karaism: a version of Torah-based Judaism that rejected the Rabbis' interpretations and advocated a more rigid and literal interpretation of the Torah.

[47] It was almost certainly the bearded G–d who wrote books for human beings to obey – therefore the 'He' that we don't believe in.

[48] This is a compilation of wise sayings by various Rabbis of Judea.

Joshua to the Elders; the Elders to the Prophets; and the Prophets transmitted it to the Men of the Great Assembly.'[49] Not only does this assert that the Torah had been given to Moses, it also makes the statement that the Torah was passed from generation to generation, culminating with the Rabbis. Crucially the same opening section concludes with three guiding principles for the Rabbis: that they should be thorough in their studies, they should establish a large body of disciples and that they should build a fence around the Torah. The first two statements are fairly straightforward but the key to the Rabbis' role and influence lay in the third: the concept of building a fence around the Torah.

If your entire worldview is based on a belief that the whole Torah has been written by G–d, then you need to be very careful to ensure that none of these G–d-given rules are ever broken (not least because many such transgressions are punishable by death!) Therefore a key role of these Rabbis and their disciples was that, after diligent study, they should come up with a series of safeguards to prevent their followers from inadvertently breaking a law of Torah (a negative commandment: 'Thou shalt not...') as well as introducing methods by which positive commandments ('thou shalt') could be effectively carried out.

---

[49] *Pirkei Avot* 1:1

Some examples. Failure to observe the rule that prohibits working on the Sabbath carries the death penalty.[50] However, the Torah does not clarify what is meant by work. So the Rabbis made a list of 39 different types of work (all the different elements required for the construction of the tabernacle in the wilderness).[51] They then elaborated on these, deciding, for example, that no musical instruments should be played on the Sabbath. This was not because of a prohibition against musical instruments per se. The thinking was that if someone played a stringed instrument on the Sabbath and a string broke, the musician might decide to mend the string. This would constitute working and would breach a law in the Torah. So no musical instruments are played on the Sabbath **just in case** a law of Torah might be broken.

A more extreme example of this is to be found in the dietary laws of milk and meat. Three times in the Torah we encounter the verse 'You shall not boil a kid in its mother's milk.'[52] Although the reason for this is not clear, it is likely that it was a cruel Canaanite practice that the early Israelite teachers were keen to prevent their people from following. The Rabbis realised that if any piece of meat was being eaten with a dairy-based sauce, in theory the meat could be the offspring of whatever produced the milk. This would represent a direct breach of a law of Torah. So, to ensure that did not happen, milk and meat should never be served together. This ruling has led to the modern Jewish practice of using different utensils for dairy and meat, and

---

[50] e.g. Exodus 31:14; also the story told in Numbers 15:32-36
[51] *Mishnah Shabbat* 7:2
[52] Exodus 23:19; 34:26; Deuteronomy 14:21

a whole raft of regulations designed to avoid this improbable occurrence. This is the 'fence' that the Rabbis are obliged to create around the Torah (taken, I would argue, to an absurd extreme).

Their other role was to devise ways in which instructions in the Torah could be acted on and brought into the daily lives of the Jews. There are many examples of this: the dimensions of a *sukkah*, the order of lighting the candles of *Chanukkah*, the instructions for the *Seder* meal to ensure it fulfils the instruction to 'tell your child' about *Pesach*, the festival of freedom.[53] Perhaps one of the clearest examples of how the Rabbis brought the Torah into the everyday lives of the Jews comes from the section of Deuteronomy known as the *Sh'ma*.[54] It says that you shall write 'these words... on the doorposts of your house.' This rather vague instruction was given tangible form by the Rabbis who effectively created the *m'zuzah*[55], chose the sections of Torah to be included in it and decided where on the doorpost and at what angle it should be located. They also decreed that the instruction to speak of those same words 'when you lie down and when you rise up' meant that the paragraph(s)[56] of the *Sh'ma* should be read in the

---

[53] *Mishnah Sukkah 1:1;* Babylonian Talmud *Shabbat 21b, Mishnah Pesachim 10*

[54] Deuteronomy 6:4-9 (also Deuteronomy 11:13-21 & Numbers 15:37-41

[55] *M'zuzah* literally means 'doorpost', but refers to the small tubular container attached to the doorpost of a Jewish house that contains a small scroll with the passages of the *Sh'ma*.

[56] *Mishnah B'rachot 1:1-4*

evening and in the morning. Needless to say, there are many pages of Talmudic debate about exactly what time in the morning these words should be said.[57]

The key thing about these decisions, legal or practical, was that the Rabbis believed that when they made their interpretations, they were not inventing these notions themselves. When G–d had written the Torah, He had known that at a certain time in history, in a particular geographical location, a particular Rabbi would make that decision based on that particular verse in the Torah. The Rabbis genuinely believed when they offered their interpretations of Torah verses they were fulfilling G–d's will. This was to become the basis of Orthodox Judaism, initially known as Rabbinic Judaism. Those who follow it would say it was a result of the Rabbis' genius and the divine inspiration that had been transmitted to them. As a Liberal Jew, I would argue it was an act of arrogance: effectively claiming to speak on G–d's behalf. But whatever one's view, there can be no doubt that it was an incredibly effective way of perpetuating the Jewish religion after the destruction of the Temple and later the banishment of the Jews from their ancestral homeland. Whatever one may think of their theology and their chutzpah, there is no doubt that the Rabbis who operated between 200 B.C.E. and 200 C.E. ensured that the religion of the Ancient Israelites, which had survived exile in Babylon to become Judaism would now continue to survive and thrive in the many lands to which the Jews would be dispersed by their

---

[57] Babylonian Talmud 'B'rachot' chapter 1

Roman tormentors. Judaism would change and adapt in the many places to which its adherents travelled, but it would always remain Judaism. The arguments over who had the most 'authentic' interpretation of Judaism would also remain.

7 - WHAT'S THE DIFFERENCE BETWEEN ORTHODOX AND LIBERAL JUDAISM?

In order to answer that question properly, it's necessary to start by defining what Orthodox Judaism is. Although its adherents would claim it began with the giving of the Torah to Moses at Mount Sinai[58] the truth is that Orthodox Judaism began with the Rabbis of Judea in Greek and Roman times. As explained earlier,[59] in order to persuade their would-be followers of the authenticity of their theology and their belief system, the Rabbis had to convince them that the first five books of the Hebrew Bible, the Torah, had been written by G–d. Not only did they successfully pull this off, they also managed to make themselves part of the ongoing process of G–d's revelation by attributing to themselves the wisdom to be able to interpret what G–d had written in the Torah – just as G–d had intended!

To be fair, the Rabbis were keen to make a distinction between the Written Torah (which was G–d's bit) and the Oral Torah (which was the Rabbis' interpretations, passed on by word of mouth until banishment meant these opinions should be recorded in the *Mishnah*). The Rabbis were kind enough to acknowledge that G–d's bit was more

---

[58] Exodus 19-20 though in fact this only describes the giving of the Ten Commandments. The suggestion that the whole Torah was given at Sinai is another Rabbinic invention.
[59] See chapter 5

important and carried more weight than theirs. Nevertheless, having made clear in the opening statement of *Pirkei Avot*[60] that there was a direct chain of transmission from the Torah that was handed to Moses down to the Rabbis of Judea, they also guaranteed their own role.

As an aside, there is a famous story in the Talmud[61] that demonstrates how the Rabbis were quite happy to overturn G–d's own rulings if the majority opinion prevailed. It tells of an argument that took place in a House of Study over a fairly minor point of Jewish law. Rabbi Eliezer took one position; Rabbi Joshua and the other scholars took another view. Rabbi Eliezer called upon various inanimate objects to prove that he was correct: he asked a tree to move, a river to flow backwards, the walls of the House of Study to bend inwards. They all did, but Rabbi Joshua refused to be moved by them. Finally a *bat kol*, a heavenly voice called out, confirming that Rabbi Eliezer's view was correct. Rabbi Joshua protested, quoting from Deuteronomy chapter 30[62], saying *'lo va-shamayim hi'* – 'it is not in the heavens!' stating that Jewish law was for the Rabbis to decide and could not be swayed by heavenly intervention. According to the Talmud, G–d laughed and exclaimed 'my children have defeated me!'

---

[60] See page 57f
[61] Babylonian Talmud *Bava Metzia* 59a-b
[62] Deuteronomy 30:12

Whatever one makes of this further act of hubris, there can be no doubt that the Rabbis established a very clear framework for the development of Judaism. It must be remembered that they constructed this framework in a hostile environment, particularly after the destruction of the Temple when the Romans continued their brutal persecution of the Jews. The Rabbis' intention, above all else, was to ensure the survival and continuation of Judaism as a living faith. The edifice they erected to protect the Torah on the one hand and to promote the practical implementation of its many laws on the other secured a future for Judaism. Their work to 're-form' (to use a provocative word) Judaism would see it flourish in future times and places that were unimaginable to these Rabbis.

They effectively created a 'bubble' within which Judaism could grow but remain true to what they perceived as its roots – the Torah that was given at Sinai. The Rabbis gave themselves the authority to interpret decrees in the Torah with enormous flexibility and licence. So in cases where a law in the Torah seemed to them to be inhumane or at least impractical, the Rabbis could introduce regulations of their own either to circumvent the law or to make it impossible to implement.

Two examples. The Torah wanted to ensure that any person who found him or herself in debt should be allowed an opportunity to be released from that debt. To enable this, it was commanded that every seventh year, all debts would be cancelled.[63] Although this law appeared to be fair, its effect was actually to increase poverty. Because they knew the debt would be cancelled a short time later, no one would lend any money from the fifth year onwards. Rabbi Hillel, who lived in the 1st century B.C.E., introduced what was known as the 'Prosbul'[64] – a vow that enabled a lender to collect debts at any time, meaning that both borrowers and lenders were protected. Although subsequent rabbinic commentators have performed academic linguistic gymnastics to demonstrate that Hillel was altering a rabbinic law, the reality is that he effectively rewrote a law in the Torah because it had become unworkable.

The second example concerns capital punishment. In many instances, the consequence of breaching a biblical law is death.[65] However, the Rabbis introduced so many conditions that needed to be fulfilled before the death penalty could be implemented: the entire incident had to be witnessed by two, independent, competent (male) adults, for example, and the tiniest doubt would be sought to prevent the ultimate punishment.

There are so many other examples of regulations that the Rabbis introduced. These make up the fabric of Jewish life: from the observance of Shabbat and festivals to

---

[63] Deuteronomy 15:1
[64] *Mishnah: Gittin 4:3, Shevi'it 10:3*
[65] e.g. breaking Shabbat laws; see note 50 p.59

regulations governing marriage and Jewish status and the laws of *kashrut*[66] and the *eruv*.[67] Every rule, every rabbinic opinion that supports and challenges it, can trace its origin back to the giving of the Torah at Mount Sinai, no matter how tortuous might be the route. It all takes place within the 'bubble' that is sustained by the unshakeable certainty that this was what G–d had intended when He wrote the Torah.

Crucially, this meant that Judaism was able to adapt itself to the variety of circumstances – geographical, social, political – in which Jews found themselves as they spread through the world of the Diaspora. In a discussion in the Talmud[68] the Rabbis consider the question of what a father is obliged to teach his son. They conclude that a boy should be taught Torah and a trade. Then, the Talmud adds: '...and some say he should teach him to swim.' If the Torah had been given at the top of a mountain in the middle of a desert, why would swimming be a priority? The answer is that in Babylon, where these Talmudic discussions took place, the river Euphrates ran through the middle of the city, and canals ran from it to virtually every street. If parents did not teach their children to swim, they would probably drown before reaching the age of six. So the

---

[66] Jewish dietary laws, based mainly on Leviticus 11, keeping milk and meat separate and slaughtering the animal as humanely as possible (*sh'chitah*)

[67] The *eruv* is a legal fiction whereby the distinction between private and public domains can be adjusted in order to permit items to be carried on the Sabbath; *Mishnah Eruvin.*

[68] Babylonian Talmud *Kiddushin 29a*

addition of swimming to this list of parental obligations was an adaptation to the local environment. A modern equivalent might be road or Internet safety. The bubble is able to stretch to incorporate new circumstances, but it remains intact.

For Orthodox rabbis making these decisions, as long as they were based on arguments conducted by earlier sages and followed the logic of Talmudic debate, they remained within the bubble of regulations implicit in the laws given at Mount Sinai. The Rabbis of the Roman era could not have known about aeroplanes or electricity, for example, but decisions made about earlier forms of transport or power were a sufficient basis for implementing G–d's will as contained in the Torah in later times.

But as soon as you suggest that its laws are outdated and that modern wisdom and common sense should be the basis of Jewish law and practice rather than the intricacies of Talmudic debate, you have stepped outside the bubble that stretches back to Mount Sinai and can extend its periphery to accommodate anything the modern age has to offer. Such steps begin with suggestions that the Torah was not written by G–d. Because once the apparently divine authorship of this document is challenged or rejected, the whole Rabbinic edifice crumbles. An Orthodox Jew will light candles at a precise time on a Friday evening because she (and her family) believe that G–d commands them to do so. A Liberal Jew will light them at a convenient time to maintain a symbolic connection to his/her tradition. The difference seems trivial, but it is enormous. The gulf between Orthodox and Liberal – or any non-Orthodox version of Judaism – is huge. One exists within the bubble that connects every action and belief to Mount Sinai. The other has stepped outside that bubble and, no matter how closely and faithfully it then adopts and carries out the rituals and practices that have developed inside it, it has effectively severed the connection with Sinai that is the essence of Rabbinic and all subsequent Orthodox Judaism.

The Impact of this dichotomy cannot be overemphasised. It may seem logical that, for example, Jews should be permitted to drive to their synagogues on Shabbat because modern demographics mean that people no longer live within walking distance. But by driving and parking around the corner, Orthodox Jews acknowledge, however hypocritically, the importance of retaining the connection between their behaviour and the rules that trace their roots to Mount Sinai. By driving into the synagogue car park, Liberal Jews, however sincere, have challenged and effectively broken that connection. Despite the obvious double standards, this Liberal behaviour is unacceptable to Orthodox Jews. And in truth, no matter how logical Liberal practices might seem, they have stepped outside the self-contained bubble of Orthodox, Rabbinic Judaism and created something different. The question is this: is Liberal Judaism an authentic development of Judaism and, if so, from where does its authority derive? For an Orthodox Jew, the answer to that question is simple: G–d decreed it at Mount Sinai. For the Liberal Jew – or any non-Orthodox Jew or Jewish movement – this remains a constant challenge.

8 - WHAT DOES A LIBERAL RABBI DO?
(A different way to read the Torah)

My basic premise, which I hope is echoed by my fellow Liberal rabbis, is that God doesn't write books. God doesn't make dramatic and fiery descents onto the top of obscure desert mountains and dictate commandments either. Let's not forget that although it contains a description of the revelation at Mount Sinai, the Torah itself does not claim that its instructions were all delivered to Moses at that time. That was an invention of the Rabbis – necessary for the continuance of the religion of Judaism, but ultimately a remarkable confidence trick that offered this ancient faith a means of survival in the many lands in which its adherents would find themselves in the ensuing centuries.

As already described, the Torah was written by human beings. In my opinion, it was a project initiated by the scribe Shaphan in the middle of the seventh century BCE to ensure that the kingdom of Judah would not disappear in the event of its capital city's destruction, as had happened to the kingdom of Israel almost a century and a half earlier. The task was twofold: to create a narrative that told of the origins of the people of Judah who would eventually be taken into captivity and a series of laws that, if implemented, might either defer this punishment or allow for a safe return. The former came from legends and tales from the people's collective memories. The latter was the work of sages and prophets, perhaps gathered and collated by the followers of the prophet Jeremiah, who was a contemporary of Shaphan. This collection of material went to Babylon with the first exile in 597 BCE, where work on it was continued by Judah's scribes and, ultimately, its priests.

According to the legend put forward in the books of Ezra, Nehemiah and Chronicles, the complete Torah was read to the people of Judah one *Sukkot* morning after the return from Babylon.[69] Even if this occurred, which is improbable, the assembled audience would probably have been rather underwhelmed. The truth is that it's not really very good. The stories of Genesis have a bit of excitement, as does the account of the escape from Egypt but it's a bit heavy going after that. The second half of the book of Exodus is mostly details of the materials used to construct the Tabernacle in the desert and their dimensions (I often refer to it as the 'Ikea Catalogue' section of the Torah). Leviticus is just a list of rules. (I once organised an evening fun activity at a rabbis' retreat where my colleagues were invited to portray the entire Torah in half an hour. The presentation of Leviticus involved one of them wrapping himself in a sheet and wagging his finger sternly while saying 'No, no, no, no no.') Numbers contains some intriguing ancient legends of the wanderings through the wilderness that includes spies, prostitutes, battles, plagues and a talking donkey. And Deuteronomy, as already explained,[70] sees Moses repeat the highlights of that journey, and gives a list

---

[69] Nehemiah chapter 8
[70] See chapter 4

of instructions about how the people should behave in the land when they enter it.

Whether or not those listeners noticed, it was fairly clear that the document had a variety of different styles, as well as a number of repetitions and inconsistencies. The astute among them would have heard, for example, that there were two different accounts of Creation. First came the well-known six day story, immediately followed by the tale that saw Adam created from the earth, followed by all the animals, all of which he named. None of them was a suitable helper for him, however, so Eve was created from his rib. The really astute listener might have noticed that the G–d doing the work of creation in chapter one was *Elohim* while the one in chapter two was *YHWH*[71] *Elohim*. No problem here if you know it's just a collection of different accounts written by people from different traditions that worshipped different gods. But if you are working on the basis that G–d wrote the whole thing, then you've got quite a lot of explaining to do...

These inconsistencies, repetitions and contradictions actually gave the Rabbis the opportunity to be creative. Assuming that every word must have been deliberately chosen by G–d when He wrote the Torah, they felt encouraged to see possibilities where something unusual occurred. One very quick example – the Rabbis decided

---

[71] See p.108 for more details about this name of God.

that the best day to marry was a Tuesday because on the third day of Creation, the line 'And G–d saw that it was good' appears twice.[72] So this day was regarded as being particularly auspicious for celebrations. This Rabbinic art of weaving stories and creating popular customs from biblical verses was known as *midrash*.[73] An enormous library of stories and explanations based on biblical verses emerged from these textual oddities, and Judaism is all the richer for them. Nevertheless, for the Liberal Jew in search of truth, there can be no doubt that the book that dwells at the heart of our Jewish heritage was written and compiled by a group of people using both their own material and that of many who came before them.

If the source of the document that formed the basis of Jewish heritage is human, then I believe the emergence of Ancient Israelite religion, and its offspring, Judaism, is all the more remarkable. Against a backdrop of fear and superstition, the prophets of Ancient Israel carved out remarkable visions of how the world should be. While those around them would regularly turn to idols, the prophets urged the Israelite people to fulfil the command of the one invisible God to establish justice in their cities. While greedy landowners gathered ever-greater amounts of land to increase their wealth, the prophets demanded that the corners of those fields be left unharvested for the poor and needy. While kings routinely sent their men into

---

[72] Genesis 1:10 & 12

[73] *Midrash* is an imaginative fictional story or explanation based on biblical verses or events.

battle every year in acts of military vanity and self-aggrandisement, the prophets foresaw a world where weapons of war would be used to produce food for all.[74]

Although they began life as proclamations by individual prophets, many of these visionary ideas found their way into the Torah, and consequently they are part of the G–d-given instruction that underpins Orthodoxy. But while the Torah lays great emphasis on the role of the priests in enabling the people to carry out G–d's will, the prophets speak out frequently against empty, meaningless ritual, emphasising instead the ethical conduct that they said ritual was supposed to inspire.

It was, you may recall, the priests who had the final say regarding the contents of the Torah.[75] When the Rabbis accorded the Torah divine authority, they were then obliged to promote that priestly view of worship, and the subservient, childlike perception of G–d that was enshrined in it. The prophets had no such limitations. Although they recognised the importance of worship, they had no doubt that it was intended to inspire worshippers to strive for greater ethical and moral heights. If it did not do this, it was indeed worthless. To be fair, the Rabbis of two thousand years ago also recognised this, and they sought to promote the ethical obligations of Judaism as well as the ritual requirements.

---

[74] e.g. Psalm 115:3-8, Leviticus 19:9-11, Isaiah 2:4
[75] See page 49

Sadly, with the passage of time, this emphasis shifted. The Jews – particularly those who lived in Christian Europe – found themselves ostracised from wider society, and were often confined to certain sections of whichever towns and cities they lived in. To an extent, they also welcomed this separation, since their intention was to preserve their identity. And they ensured that this identity was maintained by concentrating increasingly on those aspects of behaviour and practice that separated them from their neighbours, rather than looking for ways to establish mutual benefit. This in turn led to suspicion and hostility between Jews and non-Jews. Indeed it became a template for relations between faiths across the world: the main consequence of reinforcing one's own identity was the assertion of its apparent superiority vis-à-vis that of others. This was true of religion, then national identities, then political affiliation – indeed, of the entire sorry catalogue of human history. In terms of James Fowler's stages of faith development, this shows humanity stuck between stages two and three.

It has to be acknowledged, of course, that the maintaining of a people's identity was the very purpose of the Torah. And some of its contributors were quite clear that the best way to do this was to drive from the land those who worshipped other gods than that of the Israelites.[76] But among these early seekers of truth were those who could see beyond the narrow confines of individual tribal identity, who saw the compulsion to work for the

---

[76] e.g. Deuteronomy 7:1-5

betterment of all humanity, and to seek to usher in an age of peace and harmony.

It is this vision, this appreciation of a God whose demands are very different to those presented by the interpreters of the Torah from inside their bubble, that Liberal Judaism promotes. In so doing, I believe, it is possible for Judaism and any religion stuck in its own bubble to be turned from being a series of commandments issued by a G–d we don't believe in, to an obligation towards which all humanity should strive, and before which, alas, it still falls woefully short.

9 - IS LIBERAL JUDAISM JUST WATERED DOWN ORTHODOXY?

Well no, actually. To be really honest (and a bit controversial) I think it's fair to say that most Orthodox Judaism as practised in the UK is watered down Orthodoxy. By that I mean that, with the exception of the ultra-Orthodox Jews, who effectively live in their own recreated ghettos, most 'mainstream' Jews 'water down' their Jewish observance. Many who attend synagogue drive from their homes and park around the corner, pretending to have walked. They might observe some elements of *kashrut* in their homes but they will eat in any restaurant. I even knew of one Orthodox Jewish family who had four sets of crockery: one for milk, one for meat, one for Passover and one for Chinese take-away (which, I believe, included sweet and sour pork).

I realise that my opinions here will cause offence. Let me say that I am not criticising those Orthodox Jews who sincerely practice their Judaism and carry out what they regard as its obligations with honesty and integrity (though I do reserve the right to be critical of what I consider to be a flawed belief system). My observations are based on three decades of having to listen to attacks on my interpretation of my heritage from those who have no idea that their prayerbook contains requests for the rebuilding of the Temple in Jerusalem and the reintroduction of sacrificial worship or that the Torah demands that all unbelievers be wiped out.[77]

What, I wonder, does a Jew have to do or believe in order to be called an Orthodox Jew? Attend services at his synagogue every morning? (I'm assuming that this would-be Orthodox Jew is male, because in common with so many other religious traditions, women play a very secondary role in traditional Judaism).[78] Would he observe even the minor festivals and fast days of Judaism, make sure that he is home before sunset on Friday evenings in the winter, arrange his house and his life in a way that ensured none of his family breached Shabbat regulations? And would he believe that, when the Messiah comes, he, his family and all those Jews who had come before him would be gathered from their homes and their graves to be reunited in Jerusalem? Such an Orthodox Jew may find his opinions challenged by me, but I wouldn't question his sincerity.

I recall reading a Jewish Chronicle article many years ago in which a group of children asked a question of the then Chief Rabbi, Immanuel Jakobovits.[79] They asked which of the following he considered to be a more authentic,

---

[77] Deuteronomy 7:1-5

[78] Liberal Judaism, on the other hand, treats men and women as equal.

[79] Immanuel Jakobovits, 1921-1999; Chief Rabbi of the United Hebrew Congregations of the British Commonwealth of Nations, 1967-91

religious Jew: a Liberal Jew who went to his synagogue every Sabbath, served on synagogue committees and did regular work for a Jewish charity or an Orthodox Jew who only went to his synagogue at the High Holydays. The response went something like this. He said he knew what the young interviewers were trying to make him say, but in the end he'd have to say it was the Orthodox Jew. And this bit I do remember. 'Because at least he knows what it is he should be doing, even if he doesn't do it.' Strange as it may seem, I understand exactly what he meant and have no argument with it. However irreligious and non-observant the Orthodox Jew might be, his irreligiosity and his non-observance are within the bubble that holds Orthodox Judaism together. He may not be doing anything Jewish in his life, but the Judaism he wasn't doing was Orthodox and therefore authentic.

The Liberal Jew, on the other hand, has made a conscious decision to step outside that bubble. Liberal Judaism has a number of very clear fundamental starting points that separate it irrevocably from its Orthodox roots. And yes, of course it has Orthodox roots. All Judaism has Orthodox roots – the ones planted by the Rabbis who developed the Oral Torah, who traced their inspiration back to the Torah that G–d had written and given at Mount Sinai. Liberal Jews read from that written Torah every Shabbat. Liberal Jews recite prayers and observe festivals in the manner decided and decreed by those Rabbis and the ones who followed them in Babylon and Spain and Germany and wherever Jews have studied their heritage and questioned, shaped and adapted it.

But Liberal Jews have done something different. Liberal Jews have taken that heritage and questioned, shaped and adapted it with the help of enlightened, rational thought. Liberal Judaism emerged from a nineteenth century of disciplined scientific re-evaluation of old certainties. The claim that the Torah had been written by G–d was challenged, and ever more sophisticated theories emerged, stating that it had, in fact, been compiled from a variety of different sources at different times and in different places.[80] The Rabbis' Oral Torah was dismissed as a project that may have had its place in an earlier crisis, and that had developed in the largely hostile and superstitious environment in which Jews found themselves in the Diaspora. But the emergence of rational thought, bringing with it the emancipation of the Jews in Europe, and unparalleled freedom for them in America, provided the opportunity for a radical reappraisal of what were the real teachings of the ancient religion of Judaism.

Liberal Jews were no longer contained by the Rabbinic bubble that linked everything back to Mount Sinai. Liberated by critical theories about the origins of the Torah, they were free to challenge and reject some of its assertions and demands. If the commandments in the Five Books of Moses were written by people (probably men) who lived in the first millennium B.C.E., why were their insights more likely to be true or binding for their

---

[80] e.g. Julius Wellhausen, a 19th century German scholar, who set out the 'Documentary Hypothesis' in his book 'Prolegomena to the History of Ancient Israel', 1883

descendants living two and a half centuries later? The genius of the Rabbis, living under Greek and Roman rule was deemed no less archaic, and the opinions of the sages of the Talmud and other academies of the early Middle Ages were interesting from an academic or historical perspective, but not binding.

This new freedom gave licence to Liberal Jews in the 19th century to introduce reforms to their ancient faith that were as radical as those of the Rabbis had been. On one level, these 'reformers' could argue that they were simply doing what Judaism had always done: adapting their religious heritage to the times in which Jews found themselves. Indeed, they did not regard themselves as reformers at all: the name was bestowed upon them by traditional Jews who felt their adaptations were too radical, were actually undermining the Judaism they preferred. They called this version of Judaism 'Orthodox'.

The arguments between the Reformers and the Orthodox branches of Judaism raged throughout the nineteenth century and into the twentieth. The initial focal point for these developments was Germany, followed by the United States and then England.[81] Up for debate were, among other things, the role of women, the use of instrumental

---

[81] Though there was no specific German Reform movement, changes began as early as 1819; in the U.S.A. the Union of American Hebrew Congregations was established in 1883 and the Jewish Religious Union (Liberal Judaism's founder movement) in England in 1902.

music and the national language as well as or instead of Hebrew, as well as changes to the prayers relating to the Temple and the return to Jerusalem. Each of these changes led to further adaptations in other non-Orthodox congregations; each of them brought renewed outrage and protest from Orthodox authorities.

Those arguments continue to the present day. But in many ways they are futile, because of the irreconcilable difference between Judaism in a bubble (Orthodoxy) and any version of Judaism that has stepped outside it. Orthodoxy is quite clear about its roots and the source of its religious authority. Liberal Judaism lacks this clarity and certainty. Without the authority of the Rabbis there is little justification for – well, just about any Jewish practice, really. One small example: Orthodox Jews insist that Shabbat candles be kindled (by women) no later than 18 minutes before sunset on a Friday night. Liberal Jews might light candles many hours before or after sunset, according to personal convenience. Both preface the candlelighting thanking G–d for sanctifying us with divine commandments and commanding us to light Shabbat candles. Within the Orthodox bubble, that makes perfect sense. From a Liberal perspective, it is riddled with inconsistency and contradiction.[82]

---

[82] See next chapter.

From where, then, does a religious doctrine derive its authority? For Orthodox Judaism – or indeed any religion that claims to be based upon a 'divine' scripture – this is a non-question. All begins and ends with G–d as manifested in the text. For a non-Orthodox faith there are no such certainties. The question moves from the written text that has been lovingly preserved and transmitted, to the motivation and inspiration of its authors. Instead of being divine instructions and commands, the laws contained in the Torah can be regarded as a human effort to create a blueprint for a just society for a particular group of people whose identity has been shaped by their ancestors' experiences. Rather than being the final word on which all future Jewish practice and belief should be based, it is a record – inspired but deeply flawed – of a particular stage on our ancestors' journey to greater self-awareness – a journey that is ongoing.

10 - THE PARADOX OF LIBERAL JUDAISM

I recently gave a fellow rabbi[83] a recorded version of my book 'Liberal Judaism: A Judaism for the Twenty-First Century.' He was a Masorti[84] rabbi, far more traditional than me. I asked him to let me know when he had listened to the book so that we could meet and have an argument. Sadly we never had the opportunity for the argument. All I got, when he handed the CDs back to me was the statement that 'Liberal Judaism seems to know where it's come from. It's not so clear about where it's going.'

I'm pleased and proud to have written what I think is regarded as a kind of basic textbook for Liberal Judaism. Whether my other Liberal colleagues feel the same, I'm not sure. Mind you, it was written with a significant amount of input from several of those colleagues. It was constructed around Rabbi John D Rayner's 'Affirmations of Liberal Judaism' – 42 statements about the branch of the faith that had drawn me back to my heritage.[85] Those 42 were divided into two sections: 'Common Ground' (the first 22) and 'Distinctive Emphases' (the latter 20).

---

[83] Rabbi Jeremy Collick *z'l*. He had, sadly, already lost his sight when this exchange took place and passed away a matter of months later.
[84] Meaning 'traditional' – Masorti Judaism is somewhere on the Anglo-Jewish spectrum between Reform and Orthodox.
[85]http://ljoldwebsite.org/images/stories/pdf/affirmationsofliberaljudaism2006.pdf

The common ground was a pretty comprehensive overview of the basics of Judaism that are shared between all branches of Judaism. The second section dealt with those aspects of Liberal Judaism that are unique. It includes sections about how men and women are to be treated equally in synagogue life and in marriage law, how children are to have equal status in religious education and not be held responsible for their parents' actions and an inclusive attitude to Jewish identity.

These 'Affirmations' were published 90 years after the founding of the Jewish Religious Union (J.R.U.) in London. This forerunner of Liberal Judaism had a very specific agenda. Its first worship service, which was in October of 1902, took place on a Saturday afternoon, included many readings in English, and allowed men and women to sit together. One of its key movers, Lily Montagu, had written letters to many prominent English Jews inviting them to this occasion. She was encouraged by the response she received to an article she had written for the Jewish Quarterly Review in January 1899 entitled 'The Spiritual Possibilities of Judaism Today'.[86] This had prompted discussions that led to the establishment of the J.R.U. This would become the Union of Liberal and Progressive Synagogues[87] and then Liberal Judaism: a radical Jewish movement with a clear agenda that was initially shaped by Claude Montefiore and delivered by Rabbi Israel Mattuck.

---

[86] *The Jewish Quarterly Review* Vol. 11, No. 2 (Jan., 1899), pp. 216-231
[87] The U.L.P.S. was established in 1944 and rebranded to become Liberal Judaism in 2002.

Although this radical form of Judaism did not really make an impact in the U.K. until the start of the twentieth century, there had been a steady movement to reform Judaism in Germany since the second decade of the nineteenth. To a large extent this was due to the difficulties encountered by German Jews as they sought to integrate into modern German society. In the UK, the main issue that concerned Jews in the nineteenth century was enabling Jewish men to be elected to positions in government.[88] In Germany, the Jews had for centuries been regarded as inferior beings (until the late 18th century, for example, Jews were only permitted to enter the city of Berlin through the same gate used by cattle and other livestock.) The task for Jews in 19th century Germany therefore was to convince German non-Jews that they should be accepted into mainstream German society.

Initially this was achieved by adapting their form of worship to be more acceptable to German Christians (changes that went too far in the minds of some more traditional Jews, leading to a keen rivalry between Reform and Orthodox Judaism)[89]. In the second half of the century, however, as the scientific revolution galvanised European life in so many remarkable ways, Judaism took some

---

[88] David Salomons was elected to many different positions (Sheriff of the City of London, Lord Mayor of London and MP for Greenwich). Each of these elections raised the problem of a Jew being required to swear a Christian oath, which Salomons was not prepared to do. He eventually took his seat in Parliament in 1859, a year after Lionel de Rothschild, the first Jewish MP.

[89] See page 83ff.

radical steps. 1861 saw the establishment in Berlin of *die Hochschule für die Wissenschaft des Judentums* (High School for the Scientific Study of Judaism). This did not, as the name might suggest, involve experimenting on Judaism in a chemistry laboratory. Rather it signified an approach to Judaism that was rational and analytical: studying Judaism from a historical perspective and presenting it to Jews and non-Jews as a blueprint for the ideal society as set out in the visions of Israel's prophets – one that protected its most vulnerable members and that sought to establish a just and fair society in which weapons of war would be turned into agricultural tools.[90]

This tide of optimism and the belief that 'man was the measure of all things'[91] came crashing to earth in the wake of events that had come to pass before the twentieth century was even half completed. Two World Wars, the Second including the Holocaust, as well as the discovery and use of nuclear weapons, showed the extent to which human beings were capable of misusing the powers the new technology had given them. The Great Depression of the 1930s showed the pitfalls of the new economy of mass production, while the ecological impact of human industrial activity was already taking effect, even though the perpetrators did not see the seeds of the catastrophe that were being sown (and which are now becoming manifest).

---

[90] e.g. Micah 4:3
[91] Protagoras – Greek philosopher (c. 490-420 B.C.E.)

Since 1945 there have been glimmers of hope. The establishment of the Welfare State in the U.K. and of the United Nations on the global stage have undertones of the prophetic messages that resounded over two thousand years earlier. Indeed the UN building in New York carries Isaiah's visionary words of a world free of conflict.[92] But the world has not been free of conflict in the decades since World War Two. Nor has the vision of a state protecting its most vulnerable members been fully realised in this or many other countries. Had this occurred, perhaps the liberal voice, be it Jewish or otherwise, might have been able to offer praise at the implementation of the visions that underpin Liberal Judaism.

Instead, it would seem, the world has become far more self-centred. Political pronouncements in the 1980s that 'there is no such thing as society'[93] and 'greed is good'[94] have in many ways reduced human beings to consumers in a global marketplace in which few succeed and many fail, breeding new divisions between rich and poor, engendering resentment, suffering and hostility. Liberal Judaism, and indeed liberal movements in general seem to

---

[92] Isaiah 2:4

[93] Margaret Thatcher in a *Woman's Own* interview, 23rd September 1987

[94] Quote by Michael Douglas as Gordon Gekko in the film *Wall Street* (1987). Possibly not an accurate quote, but it became a kind of mantra for the new economic structure of the 1980s onwards. It could be viewed as an interesting variation on the Rabbinic view of the *yetzer ha-ra* (see chapter 11) but I believe the effect has been to create a more self-centred, acquisitive society.

have few answers to this negative and destructive worldview. Of course, there are many opportunities to offer support to those who are impoverished or rejected by this new 'society' – another archetypal element of liberalism. Liberal Judaism has been especially active in promoting the causes of refugees and those marginalised by society because of their sexuality, for example.

But as a religious movement, I believe that Liberal Judaism (as distinct from liberalism in general) has a particular responsibility to its heritage and its membership. This is a religious movement. As such it needs to base what it offers its adherents and the world in general on an awareness of God, the God initially encountered by our ancestors and who, somewhere along the way, got lost and was transformed into G-d.

The difficulty for Liberal Judaism – and any liberal approach to the search for God – is that there is inevitably a paradox at the heart of that search. If one applies rational thought to a religious question, there are two possible conclusions. Either one must accept that there can be no rational explanation for the mystery that underpins religious belief, in which case one must abandon rationality. Alternatively, one must follow the rational approach to its logical conclusion and reject belief in a divine power as being unsustainable. Either way, Liberal Judaism (along with many other similar liberal institutions) has struggled with this enigma for the last three or four decades and found a variety of answers, none of which is particularly satisfactory. For example, Liberal Judaism's watchword in the twenty-first century has been 'inclusivity'. Beginning with a strident campaign for the legal recognition of same-sex relationships and continuing with initiatives to enable people of any gender or sexuality to feel comfortable in Liberal synagogues. While this is laudable, and an integral part of Liberal Judaism must surely be this openness to all, it seems to me that this by definition can only appeal to a very limited group of people. The struggle for social justice, to which Liberal Judaism has always committed itself, is mirrored in many larger secular organisations that have no wish or need for any reference to the divine imperative that underpins their aims.

Whatever Lily Montagu envisaged in 1899, I don't think it is currently being realised or even addressed by those of us who have committed ourselves to perpetuating her message and vision. There are projects – worthy ones, for sure – but they cannot be the totality of what Liberal Judaism stands for or seeks to promote as God's message for our twenty-first century. As my colleague says, we know where we have come from, but we don't know where we are going. I believe that Liberal Judaism's role is to help humankind to rediscover faith: faith in itself, faith in the spirit that dwells within every individual, the simple faith that guided our earliest ancestors and filled them with awe. What I believe we need is a genuine faith in the potential goodness of human beings. Liberal Judaism, liberal and progressive views of the world, have begun the task of putting the 'o' back into God and rescuing religion from zealots and fundamentalists. Now we must seek to add a second 'o' to the English version of the divine name.

PART TWO

PUTTING THE 'O' IN GOD

11 - HOW BEAUTIFUL THE WORLD COULD BE

There's a passage in the current Liberal Jewish prayerbook that has always moved me. It's in the section for Holocaust Memorial Day. It goes like this:

'One evening, when we were already resting on the floor of our hut, dead tired, soup bowls in hand, a fellow prisoner rushed in and asked us to run out to the assembly grounds and see the wonderful sunset. Standing outside, we saw sinister clouds glowing in the west and the whole sky alive with clouds of ever-changing shapes and colours, from steel blue to blood red. The desolate grey mud huts provided a sharp contrast, while the puddles on the muddy ground reflected the glowing sky. Then, after minutes of moving silence, one prisoner said to another, 'How beautiful the world could be.'[95]

I'm sure each of us has had many times in our lives when we have been struck by the beauty of the world. A sunset, a mountain view, the birth of a child. The beauty of these moments needs little by way of elaboration. But I have deliberately chosen an example of the potential for the world to be perceived and acknowledged as being

---

[95] Victor E Frankl, *Man's Search for Meaning*, Hodder & Stoughton 1963, p.62-3, quoted in *Siddur Lev Chadash*, p.369

beautiful when set against the backdrop of the Holocaust. The contrast between the two extremes: the awesome beauty of nature and the staggering cruelty of some human behaviour.

As has already been noted, nature also has the capacity to inflict damage on itself – including the human beings that are part of its magnificence. But nature is a force that adheres to strict physical laws. These cannot be randomly interfered with or suspended, as the story of the plagues in the book of Exodus would have us believe. What can happen, however, is that certain elements of nature can use or adapt certain other elements of it to aid their survival and improve their way of life. There are many examples of this in the plant and animal world. But human beings have controlled, adapted, developed and exploited nature in ways far beyond the imagination of the biblical scribes, the medieval scholars who faithfully copied their words or even the 19th century academics who raised questions about their identity.

There is one element of human nature that distinguishes it from other elements of nature, even though it is very much a part of it. Like nature itself, human beings are capable of extraordinary goodness and unimaginable cruelty. Earthquakes, hurricanes, plagues and cancers happen because they can: they are a combination of unchangeable physical forces making the outcome of any critical situation inevitable. Human beings, on the other hand, have the opportunity to choose between those two extremes of goodness and cruelty. This key question of choice is perhaps the most essential of the elements that make us human. The ability we have to inflict cruelty upon fellow human beings and the world of nature is the result of a choice. The distinction between good and evil, between doing the right thing and doing the wrong thing, is the very essence of our humanity.

Jewish tradition and the scholars who created it are quite clear about this dichotomy between good and evil, clearly recognising the two extremes as integral elements of life. The prophet Isaiah, when detailing God's powers, wrote: 'I form the light, and create darkness: I make peace, and create evil: I the Eternal One do all these things.'[96] The authors of Deuteronomy[97] were similarly aware when they offered the Israelites a clear choice of which way they should behave: 'See, I have set before you this day life and good, and death and evil... I call heaven and earth to witness this day against you, that I have set before you life and death, blessing and curse: therefore choose life, that both you and your seed may live.'[98]

The Rabbis were equally clear in their depiction of the nature of good and evil, the fact that both are an essential element of nature and how, in their minds, the key

---

[96] Isaiah 45:7
[97] See page 45
[98] Deuteronomy 30:15,19

purpose of human existence was to make the correct choice between the two extremes. There are many Rabbinic quotes that address the subject[99] – it is, after all, one of the most, if not the most, vital question about our human lives: the existence of free will and the choice between good and evil.

In the opinion of the Rabbis, every human being has an evil inclination (*yetzer ha-ra*) and a good inclination (*yetzer ha-tov*).[100] The former is with every child from birth and is essentially selfish, concerned solely with the needs of the individual to survive and thrive. The good inclination, say the Rabbis, only asserts itself once children reach the age of thirteen. By that stage they are understood to have developed an awareness of the presence and the needs of others and their responsibilities towards them and the society of which they are a part. This is an ongoing process. The suggestion that human growth from childhood into adolescence and adulthood has moral and spiritual parallels has already been hinted at[101], and it is a suggestion to which I will return.[102] The point here, I think, is that Judaism has always recognised that evil is not some external force in conflict with good. Both are equally important and the key is to find the balance – or rather, to make the correct choices at any given moment of one's life. As the Rabbinic sources make clear, the evil inclination is a necessary element of human life. Without it, '... no one

---

[99] e.g. *B'reishit Rabbah* 9:7; Babylonian Talmud *Yoma* 69b
[100] Avot d'Rabbi Nathan 16
[101] See p.27f
[102] See p.119f

would build a house, or take a wife and beget children…'[103]
The key is to manage the *yetzer ha-ra*, not to seek to eradicate it.

Talking of taking wives, one of my more joyful roles as a rabbi has been to officiate at many weddings. One of the most familiar rituals is the breaking of a glass, which happens at the conclusion of the ceremony. Along with many of the rituals at wedding ceremonies in Judaism and many other religions, this custom probably has its roots in the community's desire to ward off any evil spirits intent on affecting the couple's fertility. There are many other explanations for this tradition; Rabbinic opinion connects this to the destruction of the Temple by the Romans in the year 70 C.E. Only when the Temple is rebuilt, they say, will the world once more be complete – that incompletion symbolised by the breaking of the glass.

As you can imagine, Liberal Judaism regards this rather differently. In fact, we do a lot of things differently. One of the privileges of being a Liberal rabbi is that my movement allows me to give a blessing to a couple even if one of them isn't Jewish. It usually happens immediately after the civil ceremony, which takes place while I sit in the congregation, trying not to look like a rabbi. I won't go into the details here; these are documented in many other

---

[103] Avot d'Rabbi Nathan 16

places.[104] At one such ceremony, the registrar's parting words to the couple were: 'I wish you both well. I'm sure every day will be as wonderful as today!' And off she and her colleague went.

Then it was my turn. Usually I give a little explanation about who I am and what I'm there to do, as people never quite understand why I'm there. But on this occasion I felt moved to comment on the registrar's parting words. I said something like 'I'm sorry to have to do this,' to the couple and to everyone else there, 'but I'm afraid I have to disagree with what the registrar just said. Because it seems pretty obvious to me that every day most certainly won't be as wonderful as today. Most days will be fairly ordinary. And, let's be realistic, occasionally there will be days where things are going to be a very long way from being as wonderful as today. And that is precisely why I'm shortly going to invite you to break a glass. It's to acknowledge that not every day will be as perfect as this one – there will be times of difficulty, times of struggle, times when hopes are shattered, just as the glass will be. But the glass will be broken in this context, here with your family and your friends in the hope that even at the most shattering times, it will remind you of this day and what brought you here, and it will carry you through whatever difficulty you are facing.'

---

[104] see, for example, Tobias, P *Liberal Judaism: A Judaism for the 21st Century*. Liberal Judaism, 2007

Good and evil. Blessing and curse. We cannot foresee or choose the ways in which life will test us. But we can choose how we respond to them. And we can also choose whether to make them better or make them worse (or simply to refuse to make that choice, which is equivalent to making them worse). Nature is neutral. Human beings are not. We can use our wisdom and our insight and nature's materials to create nuclear weapons. Or we can use them to create medicines that will cure cancers and whatever other challenges nature hurls at us. The choice is ours. The next chapter will explore how I believe that God – however defined – resides in that choice.

But I'd like to end more or less where I began – in the pages of a Liberal Jewish prayerbook.[105] This poem, which features on the morning of the Jewish New Year, was written by Rabbi Albert Friedlander z'l, one of my teachers and a Holocaust survivor. Once again it shows the contrast between good and evil and of our human capacity to find goodness, even in the darkest places:

'We pause in reverence before the deeds of man:
The mushroom cloud, the death camp,
The casual and cruel negligence man deals to fellow man.
But in the stillness of this questing hour

---

[105] High Holyday prayerbook: *Gate of Repentance* ULPS, London 1973 p.71-2; *Machzor Ru'ach Chadashah,* Liberal Judaism, London 2003 p.116-7

We find our way from darkness into light:
The world is beautiful. Man can be good.

May we then find the world sometimes so beautiful
That we cannot do aught but share it with a neighbour,
And may a chain reaction brighter than the light of a
thousand suns
Confront us with the inner beauty of humanity
And seal the nearness of God into our existence.' [106]

---

[106] These are the last two verses of the original version from *Gate of Repentance* before the language was altered for *Machzor Ru'ach Chadashah*

12 - WHAT WOULD A GOD FOR GROWN UPS LOOK LIKE?

That's a pretty dumb question. Because if there's one thing we can be sure of, it's that God – however perceived or defined – doesn't look like anything. Whatever is the force to which we give the name God, we can be sure it doesn't have an appearance. If it does, or if we can only envisage it as such, then it is almost certainly a manifestation of the G-d we don't believe in.

The earliest founders of the religion that would eventually become Judaism lived in a time where gods most certainly had physical appearances and features. This was a world where idols made of stone or wood were believed to possess magical powers and people would worship them and make offerings to them. Along with the demand not to oppress the stranger, the prohibition of idol worship features as the most common instruction in the Torah.[107]

Explaining the invisibility and superiority of the divine was one of the difficulties the earliest teachers and leaders of the Israelites faced. It seems that one of their first efforts to achieve this found expression in the name *elohim. El* was a basic name given to whatever power people believed supported and sustained them; *elohim* was a plural form of *el*. This seems to suggest that the Israelite

---

[107] It's the second of the Ten Commandments (Exodus 20:3-4)

God was a kind of combination of all the various gods that were being worshipped at the time.

This does not appear to have satisfied those engaged in establishing a new religion for the Israelites. Whoever came up with the next name for Israel's God created something remarkable. That name was the unpronounceable Hebrew letters *yud, hey, vav and hey.* The name may not seem to have any special qualities, but in Hebrew their significance is much clearer. Rearranging some or all of those letters give the Hebrew for 'was' (*hey, yud, hey*), 'is' (*hey, vav, hey*) and 'will be' (*yud, hey, yud, hey*). So this name of God – deliberately unpronounceable – embodies everything that ever was, is and will be. It's profound, it's mystical, it's not a God you have to choose whether or not to believe in. It just is.

The difficulty posed by such a God is obvious. We really only have one God option available to us: the G-d we don't believe in. So we either have to believe in it or we choose not to. If we do, we attend religious services and recite prayers assigning a variety of improbable powers and achievements to this God as well as occasionally asking favours of it. If we don't believe in this God then we don't really do anything, at least not in what we might call a religious way. We might do good deeds and live righteous lives, but we would neither attribute nor devote that behaviour to the God we don't believe in. But the issue here, I think isn't actually about a choice between God and no God. It's about our human inability to comprehend anything beyond the God we either believe in or we don't.

Time to focus on the Rabbis again. I have to confess that I've been a bit hard on them. I have accused them of hubris – of behaving in an arrogant manner that enabled them to claim that they possessed insight that was given specifically to them by the Almighty. In truth, this was no more outrageous than any of the other claims being made by would-be messiahs and other cultish religious groups of the time. The Rabbis recognised that first and foremost the religion they cherished and the heritage they sought to protect was in great danger. The structures they created, the 'bubble'[108] they established to give them authority, offered a version of Judaism that would enable it to survive for centuries after Jerusalem was destroyed and the Jews were dispersed to places they had never even heard of. Like it or not, they did a remarkable job, without which Judaism would have disappeared (and Christianity and Islam would never have appeared).

Even as they fashioned a structure that would ensure the survival of Judaism beyond their days, the Rabbis had a more pressing issue to address. The Jewish people were suffering extreme persecution at the hands of the Romans and were desperate for answers. Using the Torah and the Hebrew Bible as their basis, the Rabbis were able to

---

[108] See e.g. p.65

produce a quote from the sacred texts to settle any argument or prove any point.

The problem was that the vast majority of Jews at that time were simple people who wanted easy answers. In order to mollify them, the Rabbis presented them for the most part with a simplistic, almost childlike view of the G-d we now struggle to believe in. A G-d who annually records names in the Book of Life at the Jewish New Year might have been a helpful image two thousand years ago – and perhaps, for some, it still is. The suggestion that if rain has not fallen a certain time of the year, the people should fast in order to encourage it to do so[109] seems ridiculous – surely the Rabbis did not believe that such practices would influence the climate? But they lived and worked among people who did, and so, once their authority had been confirmed, they were able to exert an influence over them (a key element of the structure underpinning any religious group – the need to instil fear and exercise control).

---

[109] If no rain fell on or before the seventeenth of Cheshvan, (the 8th month – late October/early November) the learned and pious men of the community fasted for 3 days—Monday, Thursday, and Monday. In the case of continued drought, 3 more fasts were proclaimed, and, lastly, 7 fast-days on successive Mondays and Thursdays were instituted. These fasts were accompanied with many solemn ceremonies, such as the taking out of the Ark to the market-place, while the people dressed in sackcloth and placed ashes on their foreheads, and sermons were delivered (Ta'anit. 18a)

But clearly the Rabbis also had more profound insights. They wrestled with the history of their people, the situation of oppression in which they found themselves, the legacy of texts, the weight of tradition, the nature of good and evil, a sense of responsibility to the future and the place of God in all of these. In the midst of what may strike us as a series of references to and quotes from a G-d we don't believe in came the occasional brilliant insight, such as this one attributed to Shimon bar Yochai: 'If you are my witnesses, says the Almighty, then I am God. But if you are not my witnesses then I am, so to speak, not God.'[110]

The vital implication in this remarkable statement that is almost two thousand years old is effectively the existence of God is dependent on human recognition of the divine. If that is the case, then it would appear that God is slowly withdrawing from our world as increasing numbers of people reject God's existence. But, as already argued, this absent God is the G-d we don't believe in: the G-d of the Hebrew Bible who brought rain and to whom sacrifices were dutifully (and, from the Divine perspective, pointlessly) offered, and His various successors, which were more a reflection of human need than a divine presence. These versions of 'God' were of human creation, a response to the world in which our various ancestors found themselves. They were shaped by the cultural, social, geographical and theological environment in which

---

[110] *Sifrei* Deuteronomy 346

those ancestors were located. The God(s) we don't believe in were made by human beings.

'God' cannot exist without us. Whether or not we created God is moot. We contain God and God is in us. This is a God for grown ups. This, I think, is the place to return to James Fowler's stages of faith development. Having taken this lengthy detour to explore what human beings – specifically Jewish ones, but others too – have done to God and the world, we can now consider Fowler's fourth stage. He calls this the 'individuative-reflective' stage, which is where people start to see beyond their own belief system and recognise other systems. This is a tough stage, says Fowler, often started in early adulthood. These people often reject their own faith after subjecting it to critical analysis. This is actually a step forward in terms of developing faith, though it often appears – and feels – like a retrograde step. Level five is called 'conjunctive faith', a stage where people realise the limits of logic and start to accept life's mystery. They often return to their original faith stories and symbols but are no longer restrained or limited by their theological restrictions. The sixth stage, 'universalising faith', is attained only by a few individuals but, says Fowler, those attaining it live their lives to the full in the service of others with no real worries or doubts.

Enough time has been spent considering the G-d we don't believe in, who clearly dwells in the lower regions of Fowler's scale. What interests me here is that the higher levels are clearly more concerned with how the individual sees the world and acts within it. The implication is that

God is experienced and encountered through dedication to the service of others. Is that the answer? Does a spiritual journey take us from selfishness to selflessness? If this is true, then presumably God dwells in us and is manifested through our interaction with others. Is this a God we can believe in? And is this a God to whom it is possible – or even necessary – to pray? More questions than answers here. But perhaps a grown-up attitude to God emerges from these questions. Good deeds – *mitzvot* – are actions for the benefit of ourselves and those around us, not private ritual deeds ostensibly commanded by the G-d we don't believe in. God dwells in us and in the effect we have on others. That is a God for grown-ups. And the role of Liberal Judaism – indeed every religion worthy of that name – must surely be to encourage us to grow to understand how to appreciate and serve that God.

13 - IS GOD A VERB?[111]

It's time for a re-evaluation of what is actually meant by 'God'. Of course, since God cannot really be defined, the only way to begin such a venture is by detailing what God isn't.

Which brings us back rather nicely to old Mrs Cohen from chapter three. Perhaps she's still sitting at the back of the synagogue, uttering her weekly prayer to be able to win the lottery. Asking the G-d we don't believe in to do something impossible. Or maybe she took some time to think about what that G-d meant when He asked her to buy a ticket.

I like to think that 'buying a ticket' to give God a chance is connected to James Fowler's 'stages of faith' chart, or something that equates to it. In order to gain from the attempt at an encounter with the divine that dwells within and all around us, we need to be prepared to abandon the self-centred and superstitious notions that we invariably and inevitably bring to the religious experience.

---

[111] I was initially genuinely proud of this chapter title, which I thought was original and was considering as a title for this book. Research has revealed at least 3 other books with titles that are variations on it, however. Ah well...

Of course, it isn't the fault of the worshippers that their expectations are rooted in the lower levels of the stages of faith. Everything about organised religion places them there and keeps them there. The pedantic, almost obsessive nature of the symbols and rituals that are part of any formal worship service. The paternalistic nature of the prayers that remains, no matter how many adaptations might be made to liturgy in a self-conscious and therefore clumsy manner. The improbability and occasional absurdity of the statements made about and the requests addressed to the G-d we don't believe in.

Clinging to a belief in these, it could be argued, leaves us unable to move beyond the second or third stages of spiritual development according to Fowler's chart. We are either children, behaving like Mrs Cohen and constructing our faith around the G-d we don't believe in, or we are mocking her naïve faith as we reject it with the fervour of adolescent rage. At this point, although there may be benefit for some in such comforting beliefs, we are some distance from the higher stages of spiritual possibility. As we pass into adulthood in the eyes of the society in which we now take our place, the likelihood is that we cease to engage in a search for meaning as material needs and obligations overwhelm us. Thereafter we remain, for the most part, trapped in a place where we either hold onto or reject what we believe to be the main tenets of the religion with which we grew up. At the same time, we recognise the need to balance that religious heritage with a world less secure and certain, more complicated and threatening than that of our childhood.

There will always be moments in our lives when we are given pause to contemplate the possibility of greater meaning, when we are forced to confront the fundamental mystery at the heart of existence. It's no coincidence that the stages of our human life cycle – birth and death in particular, but also coming of age and marriage – are occasions when even the most outspoken disbelievers (in the G-d we don't believe in) are drawn to their religious heritage. Many are the ceremonies I have conducted at these various moments in congregants' lives or those of their children, attended by family members who vaguely recognise a few of the Hebrew words or prayers being uttered, but whose emotional connection to their Jewish heritage feels tenuous and half-forgotten.

Of course there are other connections that are more readily observable. Jewish food for example – and I'm talking about bagels and smoked salmon, not the religious laws of *kashrut*. Or attitudes towards the State of Israel, and the lazy connection often made between anti-Israeli sentiment and anti-Semitism. But those are cultural and political bonds; they are separate from and even actively dismissive of the emotional and spiritual connection between Jews, their Jewish heritage and the Jewish God. And there is an extent to which even those who enthusiastically embrace and follow the Rabbinic rules and regulations (or whatever is their interpretation of them) are not genuinely connected with the Divine. They are devoting their lives to the G-d we don't believe in. Their way cannot be our way. They are obedient children, following a religion. We are questioning and questing grown ups, searching for an awareness of God.

Part of the problem, I think, lies in the word 'God'. It's so full of preconceived ideas and prejudices that as soon as the word gets mentioned, any chance of a meaningful discussion about it and what it signifies is lost. Maybe the Ancient Israelites had it right: give the Divine a name that can only be pronounced by one person and insist on pain of death that this one person is only ever allowed to utter it three times in a special place once a year. It was clearly important: it is the third of the Ten Commandments,[112] three places above 'You shall not murder'[113].

But more important than what to call it or not to call it, I think, is how to approach it. I'm not talking here about understanding or defining 'God' – I once wrote of the futility and even danger of attempting to do so. 'I think God is actually in the question. The kind of question that asks for guidance, that asks for explanations, that asks for help, that asks for reasons. The real challenge, I think, is to go on asking the questions. Because as soon as we think we have found the answer, we might become complacent, self-satisfied – dogmatic even – as we cease to ask the question and seek merely to convince ourselves and others of the correctness of our answer. That is precisely the point

---

[112] Exodus 20:7, Deuteronomy 5:12 'Do not take the name of the Eternal One your God in vain.'
[113] Exodus 20:11, Deuteronomy 5:17 'You shall not murder.'

where God becomes absent from our religion, our world and our lives.'[114]

This isn't about defining God, though, it's about finding God – a grown up version. Let's take another look at James Fowler's Stages of Faith. They talk of childhood and adulthood in a way that coincidentally seem to resonate with my idea of child-like and grown-up views of God. The key conclusion that Fowler makes is that the journey to and through the higher stages requires recognition of the limitations of all faith systems and acknowledgment of the 'paradoxes in life'. Those few who attain the sixth and final level, '...live their lives to the full in service of others without any real worries or doubts.'[115]

How nice it would be to be able to live life without worries or doubts! The key phrase, however, is 'in service of others'. The suggestion that true spiritual awareness manifests itself in dedication to improving the lot of other people in whatever context offers a very different – and very profound – understanding of the Divine. I think it comes back to the distinction between the *yetzer ha-tov* and the *yetzer ha-ra* – the good and bad inclinations we all possess. Perhaps those could be redefined as selflessness and selfishness. The more selfish one is, the more one is listening to and heeding the dictates of the *yetzer ha-ra*.

---

[114] Tobias, P. Why Am I Here? (Kindle Locations 201-206). 2012, Kindle Edition.
[115] Fowler, James W. 'Stages of Faith', Harper & Row, 1981

The more selfless, the more one is responding to and acting on one's good inclination.

The Rabbinic concept of *mitzvah* comes into play here. Often mistranslated in our modern world as 'doing a good deed', a *mitzvah* is actually a divine commandment. So in traditional Judaism, helping someone out of poverty or caring for them when they are sick has the same value as putting on *t'fillin*[116] or reciting a particular prayer at the correct time. This is patently nonsense. I would suggest that the latter is self-indulgent, and is a manifestation of a childlike approach to the G-d we don't believe in. I would even go so far as to say that it is selfish: it serves no one except the individual who believes they are earning favour in the eyes of G-d. The selfless *mitzvah*, on the other hand, quite clearly benefits others and would be far more pleasing to God, even if it's the one we don't believe in.

But perhaps it isn't about 'pleasing God'. The G-d we don't believe in probably has, in the imagination of those who obey and carry out that G-d's ritual 'commandments', a kind of score sheet on which are detailed records of individual acts. This is the kind of attitude that was derided by the prophets of Ancient Israel, who repeatedly insisted that God had no wish for such empty acts. 'For I desire love, not sacrifice,' said Hosea[117] while Amos insisted that

---

[116] Phylacteries containing the words of the *Sh'ma*, Deuteronomy 6:8, 11:19; Numbers 15:37-41
[117] Hosea 6:6

God wanted to see 'justice roll down like waters, righteousness like an everflowing stream.'[118] Such an approach has little need for 'believing'. It is about doing.

So perhaps the way to see a grown up God – or whatever we might call the Divine – is to regard it as being a verb, a form of action. I don't think that the concept of 'godding' will ever catch on. But let's regard 'God' as being present when people are behaving and acting in a way that seeks and actually brings improvement to the life of an individual or a community or society as a whole. This 'God' can be seen as a manifestation of the potential we each possess, as exemplary action by our *yetzer ha-tov,* a triumph of good over evil if you like, but that sounds a bit sanctimonious. It doesn't really matter. That's all small print on the back of the ticket God asked Mrs Cohen to buy. The important thing is to have the ticket and recognise that its purpose is to encourage – or demand even – that to serve God (a very cryptic concept) is actually all about serving others (much easier to grasp and to do). The function of religion – a function that it achieves ever more infrequently – is to encourage and inspire us to do that. 'God' – or whatever we are going to call him/her/it – dwells in the performance of that service to, that respect and love for, other people. It's about being – and doing – 'Good'.

---

[118] Amos 5:24

14 – A TIME FOR GROWING

This poem, from Robert Frost, features in the Liberal High Holyday prayerbook[119]:

God of pity and love, return to this earth.
Go not so far away, leaving us to evil.
Return O God, return. Come with the day.
Come with the light, that we may see once more
Across this earth's uncomfortable floor
The kindly path, the old and loving way.
Let us not die of evil in the night.
Let there be God again. Let there be light.

When I started writing this book, I wasn't entirely sure where it would take me. After almost three decades as a Liberal rabbi, during which time the world has lurched from crisis to crisis (as have I, but that's a different story) and, despite the excellence of its teachings, its visions and its message of hope for humankind and the planet on which it dwells, Liberal Judaism has failed to gain traction in the minds or actions of many. The same is true of other liberal faiths, while those offering extreme (and often aggressive) solutions seem to be thriving.

---

[119] From Sonnet XIII, Robert Nathan, 'Selected Poems' (1935) in *Machzor Ru'ach Chadashah*, p.96

Needless to say, there have been many occasions during my three decades en route to and in the rabbinate when I have encountered many doubts and my faith – both in my Jewish heritage and in the human race as a whole – has been tested. The attack on the World Trade Center in 2001, Israel's actions in Gaza and the West Bank, the ongoing civil war in Syria and the displacement of so many millions – these and countless other examples of human cruelty and stupidity make it clear that the optimism of the early 20th century has been replaced by something very different a hundred years later.

One thing has sustained me through the years of my rabbinic career despite the frustration caused by human behaviour at a variety of levels. The people whom it has been my privilege to meet, to guide, to teach and to support at every stage along the way. When my father challenged me on my decision to become a rabbi in the mid-1980s, he asked two penetrating questions. The first – with which I have been struggling ever since – was 'what is your understanding of God?' The second, which I found rather patronising at the time, followed on from my explanation that much of my work as a rabbi would be focused on the community that would one day employ me. 'So you'll be a kind of social worker with God?' he asked, with no little sarcasm in his voice. I emphatically denied his suggestion (more of an accusation!) but perhaps it's time to reflect on that statement again.

According to an online dictionary, a social worker is 'a person who is trained to help people who are at a mental, physical, economic or social disadvantage.'[120] I suspect there are several politically incorrect observations that could be made there about members of the Jewish community. If I was really going to be a social worker, with or without God, it might appear that there are many communities significantly more in need of support in those fields than the ones I have served in Birmingham, Glasgow and Elstree.

But I think that whole human race is, or should be, engaged in an effort to improve itself and take steps to fulfil its potential. And it doesn't really matter where individuals are at any given stage of their development or the development of the society in which they live – they can always move on. If the role of religion is to provide meaning, purpose and direction to life (and I think, at its heart, that's what religion is and should be), then it doesn't matter what is the starting point. It's the momentum and the trajectory that matters.

I recall an incident in the very first days of my rabbinic career. It was at the Birmingham Progressive Synagogue in the early 1990s. A group of Christian students from a local theological college had visited the synagogue for a Shabbat morning and after the service, I invited them to look at the Torah scrolls in the ark. One of them was a little diffident about stepping onto the *bimah*, the rostrum at the front of

---

[120]https://dictionary.cambridge.org/dictionary/english/social-worker

the synagogue to approach the ark. "Isn't this holy?' he asked, rather nervously, perhaps recalling biblical incidents where entering certain restricted spaces often resulted in the spectacular extermination of unauthorised trespassers. 'No,' I laughed. 'This is just stuff. It's not holy. We, people, we are the ones that are holy.'[121]

A Jewish congregation is known in Hebrew as a *k'hillah k'doshah,* usually translated as 'a holy community.' There's something that has always infuriated me about the way the Hebrew word *kadosh* is translated. The common translation is 'holy', a word that has Christological connotations and for me conjures up images of angels and haloes. Its original meaning is 'separate' or 'distinct'. In the Hebrew Bible, that which was *kadosh* was 'set aside' for God; its status changed from being common and everyday into something that was the provenance of the Divine. So a sentence like *'K'doshim tih'yu ki kadosh ani Adonai eloheichem'*[122], usually translated as '...you shall be holy because I the Lord your God am holy,' should actually read '...you shall be distinct, because I, *YHWH*[123] am separate from, different to you.' That's a very different meaning and

---

[121] Remarkably, shortly after writing this, I received an email from one of those Christian visitors, who fondly recalled that day more than a quarter of a century ago. He is now considering conversion to Judaism and wrote 'I certainly wanted you to know of my gratitude to you and the people of Birmingham Progressive Synagogue for showing me what real welcome and inclusion looks like.'

[122] From Leviticus 19:1

[123] That which was, is and will be (currently translated in LJ prayerbooks as 'The Eternal One') – see page 108f

offers, I think, a far more acceptable and accessible approach to the concept of what we still tend to refer to as 'holiness'.

So every member of a Jewish community – indeed every member of the human race – is *kadosh* – distinct and special. It's a view that is often hard to sustain in such a crowded, busy world where we often find ourselves surrounded by strangers in so many different situations. How can we bring a religious message to such people? How can we aspire to reach the top level of Fowler's stages of faith, where we recognise that all people are equally worthy of respect and – yes, I'll use the word – love? I think it's a lot easier than we realise...

Rabbi Leo Baeck[124] once said: 'One can always find warm hearts who in a glow of emotion would like to make the whole world happy but who have never attempted the sober experiment of bringing a real blessing to a single human being. It is easy to revel enthusiastically in one's love of humanity, but it is more difficult to do good to someone solely because they are a human being.'[125] He's right of course. That's why when we walk along a busy street, we look at the ground below us and, if we look up

---

[124] Dr Leo Baeck (1873-1956) German rabbi, scholar and theologian. Survivor of the Holocaust and gave his name to the college that trained me as a rabbi.
[125] Quoted in *Forms of Prayer,* Reform Synagogues of Great Britain, 1977, p386

and notice someone looking at us, we avert our gaze with an uneasy sense of shame.

I have recently taken to engaging in the kind of experiment to which I think Leo Baeck is alluding. I walk through the streets looking at people. Often they avert their eyes like I used to do and like, I suspect, most of us do. But those whose eyes meet mine receive a nod or a smile – even a greeting. Often that is reciprocated. But even if it isn't, it doesn't matter. By attempting that contact, I have taken the first step to break down a barrier. And it doesn't stop there. With a fervour that sometimes confounds me, I find myself almost constantly on the lookout for opportunities to perform an act of kindness – at train stations or in supermarkets.

I'm not going to give specific examples, because they will sound trivial and ridiculous. And I have to confess that having spent many chapters considering the history and the purpose of religion, and the nature of God in our world, it feels faintly ridiculous to arrive at the conclusion that the key expression of faith dwells in being nice to strangers. What's even worse is that I often feel good about myself for behaving in this ostensibly altruistic manner – something that up to now has made me feel guilty, because it stops being altruistic and becomes selfish.

But I've recently come to the conclusion that's okay. And the truth is that the more I engage in this practice, the less I feel the need to congratulate myself. It is gradually becoming a part of who I am. Of course, random acts of kindness are hardly a new concept. Many are the opportunities to bring a little goodness into the life of someone else. Coffee chains are now enabling customers to buy a 'suspended' coffee in addition to their own: a cup of coffee that can be given to a homeless person at some later point. Such acts of kindness are the exception in our society, but they stand in stark contrast to the selfishness and greed, the arrogant and immoral wielding of power and acquiring of wealth that seems to fill our daily news bulletins. But suppose it wasn't 'random'? Suppose it became a conscious and deliberate effort to bring kindness into our communities, onto our streets, into the lives of all those with whom we have the opportunity to connect, and whom we so often pass wordlessly by?

So my conclusion at the end of this journey is that the way to find meaning and purpose in life is through behaving kindly to others. That can be helping random strangers as an individual, or organising and galvanising one's community to take part in more structured acts of generosity and kindness. It also manifests itself in establishing supportive relationships within any given community – and for me it has been a privilege to help and guide members of the congregations I have served through key moments in their lives in my career as a rabbi.

And that, I believe, is how we bring God into our lives. Or rather, how we 'do' God in our lives. God is a verb. And by 'doing' God, we turn God into Good. When we pray, we are not hurling words at a dispassionate sky. We are addressing ourselves, challenging ourselves to behave in a way that will enable us to connect – however briefly – with other human beings in ways that are mutually beneficial. This is how we can grow, this is how we can aspire to reach the higher levels of faith. No one wants or expects us to be Mother Theresa. But as the well-known rabbinic story goes: 'Before his death, Rabbi Zusya said, 'In the world to come they will not ask me: 'Why were you not Moses?' They will ask me: 'Why were you not Zusya?'[126] We should strive to be the best people we can be, by seeking to bring all the goodness we can into the lives of others. In this way, I believe, we take a step further on the human journey to spiritual maturity, recognising that religion only has merit when it encourages and inspires us to be effective in the world as we seek to bring God – to bring Good – into our lives and the lives of others.

---

[126] Quoted by Martin Buber in *Tales of the Hassidim: The Early Masters,* Shocken Books 1968, p. 141.

15 - MAKING IT REAL

The problem with religion and theology and – let's be honest – even God (with or without an 'o' or even two in the middle) is that it's all theoretical. Full of words but ultimately without any practical substance. Moreover, in our cynical world, it's easy, almost fashionable, to make fun of seriously stated opinions or beliefs.

Back in Chapter One I made reference to Professor Richard Dawkins.[127] We had a public conversation following a showing of the film he produced with Laurence Krauss. It was a particularly dreadful film in which, to prove the authenticity of their strongly atheist beliefs, they interviewed the most extreme fundamentalist Christians. These interviewees were, naturally enough, keen to try to persuade Dawkins of the authenticity of the G-d we don't believe in. Needless to say, he was unconvinced. I would imagine the entire audience at that screening – including me – were not convinced either.

There was a section of the film that reported on an open-air festival celebrating atheism, at which Dawkins, Krauss and others gave speeches extolling the virtue of not believing in a deity, rather like pop groups performing their greatest hits to an admiring audience. It was called the

---

[127] p.15

'Reason Rally' and it took place in Washington DC on March 24th 2012. It has been called the 'Woodstock for atheists and sceptics'.

The adoring crowd at this event shared food and beverages, clapped and cheered their heroes, even followed Lawrence Krauss around, asking to shake his hand. They braved heavy rain (one can imagine what religious fanatics would have had to say about who or what mischievous deity arranged the weather!) and, for the duration of this event, formed a community with a shared interest. I have no access to individual anecdotes, but I'm sure many friendships were formed, much food was shared and plenty of support was offered and received in a variety of ways. In other words, there would have been an abundance of opportunities for my definition of God – the potential for and realisation of goodness – in places where human beings interact.

My point is, I suppose, that you don't need to believe in the existence of a supernatural deity with His variety of improbable attributes to be able to put into practice the ability (and even the obligation) human beings have to bring goodness into the world. You just need an opportunity to do it. And the establishment of any community with a shared interest or a common goal has the capacity to generate that goodness and cultivate an environment that facilitates and encourages it.

The problem with many of these communal groupings is that their very raison d'etre is to provide opposition to an already existing group. Nothing focuses the human mind more keenly, it would seem, than the presentation of an individual or group with views or policies to which it is fashionable or expedient to object. Human history is replete with examples of our capacity to revel in our opposition to something and our painful reluctance – inability even – to find ways to co-operate for the common good. I am pleased to have the opportunity to turn to Monty Python's Life of Brian to illustrate this point. In the scene where the people have just decided that Brian is the Messiah, one person objects and says that is not the case. Brian's 'followers' respond to John Cleese's demands to 'persecute the unbeliever' and the mob descends on this individual, ignoring the cries of Brian – the very Messiah whose words they have just decided to follow – to leave him alone.[128]

Nevertheless, whatever the purpose or unifying factor of a particular group might be, there will always be an opportunity, and a need, for that sense of community that is such a basic element of our humanity. As the Liberal Jewish High Holyday prayerbook reminds us when it looks to the earliest days of human development:

---

[128] Monty Python's Life of Brian, HandMade Films; Python (Monty) Pictures, 1979

'You gave us wit
to fashion tools to meet our needs,
and the power of speech, that magic gift
by which each soul, unique and separate,
yet shares its life with others,
so that the distance between human beings
is bridged by sympathy and understanding.

Thus it came about that, though each individual,
unaided and alone, is weak and helpless,
Your gift of love has taught us
the art of living with our fellow men and women,
in one humanity.'[129]

God's gift of love may have taught us the 'art of living with
our fellow men and women in one humanity' but we have
used our other gifts to create division and hostility, fear
and suspicion. We have cultivated societal structures and
economic systems based on levels of selfishness and greed
that seem to contradict and legislate against that
possibility.

As a consequence of our current political, social,
environmental and even psychological state, we now
struggle to find meaning and direction in a world
overcrowded with such divisions and people striving to

---

[129] *Machzor Ru'ach Chadashah*, p.295

come to terms with them. Never has the call for a world view based on tolerance and mutual understanding been more urgently needed. And never, it would seem, has the possibility of the implementation of that 'art of living' seemed more distant or remote.

I believe that a rediscovery of a genuine understanding and awareness of God is the key to our human future. Not the G–d of countless religious movements where the performance of elaborate rituals, the repetition of archaic and impossible beliefs and the ministering demands of hypocritical leaders serve only to drive God from the world. I am talking about the establishment of communities in which the ability to identify shared needs and goals is cultivated without a need to find an opposition on which to focus. Communities that are constructed on a yearning to provide comfort and support, encouragement and opportunity for human beings to discover the fellowship and unity of purpose of which we are capable.

This is all very broad and idealistic. The conclusion of this journey to discover the role that God can and should play in our twenty-first century lives must have some specific recommendations, otherwise it will have been pointless. Interesting and entertaining, I hope, but unless it offers a direction and a possibility, it wasn't really worth writing – or reading.

At the start of the twenty-first century, there was a recognition by Jewish communal leaders in the United States that the standard model of synagogues wasn't working. It was typified by a woman who resigned her membership of a large congregation after twenty years of regular attendance. She explained her sudden departure to the puzzled rabbi, saying 'I have been a member here for twenty years. I have attended all the major synagogue events. And I have never met anybody.' Other rabbinic commentators have also noticed the tendency of modern synagogues to create smaller interest groups, breaking the community into parts by age, gender or some other distinction:

'This breaking apart of community into marketable groups, an overwhelming amount of programming aimed at serving these niches, and zero connectivity between these disparate parts is going to destroy Jewish life. The worst part is, it ignores the whole reason why people get involved in Judaism and Jewish life in the first place...

The rabbi[130] then continues, in bold letters: **'It's the people. The people are who matter.'** He adds '... And if we don't step away from the calendar, step away from the boardrooms where we discuss the age-old question of "how do we get blah blah blah to our programs?" and

---

[130] Rabbi Patrick Beaulier, in a blog I once found on his 'Punk Torah' website but can no longer locate (http://punktorah.org/rabbi-patrick-beaulier/).

instead ask: "How are we doing as a community to serve other people?" "How can we help create the kind of world that others want to live in?" ...then this enterprise called Judaism is completely screwed.'

Communities exist to enable people to connect with other people. And when people come together, the possibility emerges of their being able to show kindness to, and receive kindness from, others. As I hope I have demonstrated, when people make the effort to bring goodness into the lives of others, they also bring it into their own lives. The creation of a mutually supporting community, regardless of its purpose, can embody and exemplify the presence of God, the generating of Goodness that is possible between all human beings.

Over a decade ago, 'Mitzvah Day' began in the UK.[131] It's an archetypal 'Goodness' project, where thousands of people from different religious and non-religious communities combine to perform a range of different acts of kindness, responding to a variety of communal, environmental and social needs. But my vision of the Good we can do to bring God into our everyday lives doesn't have to be – indeed cannot be – limited to one day every November.

---

[131] Founded by Laura Marks in 2005, this is an annual one-day event in which many Jewish, and latterly other, religious communities take part.

In the context of Liberal Judaism, this can best be achieved by regarding our synagogues as places designed specifically to foster and achieve that. As already mentioned, a congregation is a *k'hillah k'doshah* – a gathering of people that is *kadosh* – separate or distinct. One way that distinctiveness can manifest itself is through the creation and cultivation of an environment that, by its attitude and its actions, can generate the possibility of the Goodness that is God. Or of the God that is Goodness. Because they are interchangeable. The key to a Liberal Jewish future that can benefit its members and bring hope to a troubled world is, I believe, to encourage us all to behave in a more kindly fashion to ourselves and each other: in our communities, and in our everyday lives to remind ourselves and one another of the possibility of God.

That's a long way from the G-d we don't believe in who appears in the prayerbooks and Torah readings and discussions and education programmes with which we fill our synagogues. Of course, such things have been the essence of Jewish life since before the first synagogue was established over two thousand years ago. But at the heart of these ventures there have always been people seeking to find common ground and establish contact with others with whom to share their interests, their enthusiasm, their concerns, their lives. This is true of any human community: there is nothing uniquely Jewish or Liberal about this.

But this book is written by a Liberal Rabbi for an assumed audience of Liberal Jews looking for a definition of God and a sense of direction in a seemingly godless and directionless world. And if I need to present my conclusion of wrestling with the enormities and the inconsistencies, the depth and the contradictions of Jewish history as contained in its texts and its traditions, then let it be this. Finding God is about finding in ourselves the ability and the potential to bring goodness into the lives of others. That's it.

AFTERWORD

When I first began writing what eventually became this book, I really had no idea where it was taking me. I just knew that I had several issues with the direction that Liberal Judaism seemed to be taking and a sense that a new theology was needed. I didn't imagine that I was going to be able to do any more than outline my concerns; a kind of soon-to-retire series of reflections on what, perhaps, I had hoped I might see or even achieve in my rabbinic career. I deliberately made each chapter 'sermon' length in case, if nothing else, they might come in useful for that purpose.

Then, after I'd written about four chapters, I came across a Twitter thread from Rabbi Danya Ruttenberg. It was about stages of spirituality or faith development; a progression suggested by James Fowler in the early 1980s. It seemed to fit with where my thinking was heading – that human beings were stuck in a kind of adolescent phase with regard to their understanding of or relationship with God. I felt that a grown up attitude to God was needed, but I couldn't work out what that might be.

So I thought that these stages of faith development might provide a direction for my thoughts. But as I read through the stages, I was hugely underwhelmed with his conclusion of what constituted the highest level of faith and spiritual

141

maturity. As mentioned on page 112, the pinnacle of faith development is the devotion of one's life to the service of others. When I first read it, this struck me as rather banal: I felt as though the human striving to discover God ought to be more than living an altruistic life dedicated to the service of others.

Yet at its heart, the basic message of the Torah, expressed in Deuteronomy and repeated through the book of Kings, is the demand (or at least the hope) that human beings will choose good over evil. That theme is reiterated by the Rabbis and reappears frequently in Jewish literature throughout the centuries. So whatever is divine in human potential resides in this obligation – or opportunity – to acknowledge God by choosing to do good.

This seemingly simple conclusion was reflected in my own behaviour in the world, my own choice. Once again, the details of my actions seem trivial and banal: I smiled at people in the streets, I help young mothers or elderly people struggling to deal with their shopping baskets or trolleys, I even spent 20 minutes driving an elderly person around a car park at a large shopping outlet to track down the forgotten location of the car. This is a long way from Carl Sagan's definition of God in chapter one as 'the set of physical laws that govern the universe'. It sounds trivial and trite to place a definition so profound alongside something as simple as smiling at someone in the street.

But I think it works. It's different from Sagan's 'God'. The physical wonder of the universe is indeed something at which to marvel – even if we don't call it 'God'. But the bond that connects two human beings when one makes a conscious choice to extend a hand to another – particularly if they are strangers – is no less wonderful. Indeed, it can often be more wonderful. The more immediate and practical such goodness is, the more effective and real it is. Of course fighting for social justice is important. Of course promoting inclusivity is important. But I believe that the most immediate way to bring God into the world and our everyday is not by waving placards or creating gender-neutral prayers. That can be achieved by turning God into Good. Doing good enables God. Doing good is doing God. God and good are one and the same. That is a theology, a God, worth believing, following and promoting.

'For this commandment that I am commanding you today is not too difficult for you, nor is it too remote. It is not in heaven that you might say 'Who will go up to heaven for us to fetch if for us and make it known to us that we might understand it?' Nor is it across the sea that you might say 'Who will go across the sea for us to fetch if for us and make it known to us that we might understand it?' No. This thing is very close to you – on your lips and in your hearts that you might do it.'

Deuteronomy 30:11-13.

APPENDIX

JAMES FOWLER'S STAGES OF FAITH DEVELOPMENT

STAGE ONE Intuitive-Projective	Pre-school age: children pick up basic ideas about God from parents, the community in which the parents participate (or not) and from external influences (children's books, TV, society). Their general ideas tend to be a mixture of fantasy and reality, so concepts of God are simple and personal.
STAGE TWO Mythic-Literal	Primary school introduces more logical concepts to children's thinking. They tend to believe literally the stories to which they are introduced at school and in their faith community or wherever they encounter them. This literal belief in stories – and the rituals and symbols that accompany them – often remains unchanged all the way into adulthood, producing a child-like approach to God and religious or other beliefs.
STAGE THREE Synthetic-Conventional	Reaching one's teenage years brings a need to combine the various groups and milieus in which life occurs – school, family, other social groupings. The teenager attempts to make sense of this by developing a broader belief system to incorporate these differences. Although it might seem like an all-embracing world-view, it is nevertheless rooted in their original belief system. In this stage, groups or people who hold and promote those beliefs are regarded as authority figures. Many people remain in this stage throughout adulthood, vaguely adhering to the beliefs of the group in which they grew up, without necessarily realising that they are doing so.

STAGE FOUR Individuative-Reflective	This stage might be reached in early adulthood, if one has not become stuck in stages 2 or 3. The limitations and even contradictions of the faith in which they grew up are highlighted by a growing awareness of the existence of other interpretations of the world. Their original faith is challenged and often rejected. To outsiders – particularly those stuck in stage 3 – this may seem like a backward step in terms of belief but it is, in fact, a critical and maturing stage of faith development.
STAGE FIVE Conjunctive Faith	There is no specific age at which this stage is or might be reached. It is where the limits of a rational approach to life's mysteries have become apparent. The questions and challenges raised by such realisations often lead to a return to the stories and rituals of their faith but without the unwavering adherence demanded by stage 2 or the limitations of stage 3.
STAGE SIX Universalising Faith	According to Fowler, few people reach this stage. It involves dedicating one's life to the service of others, apparently without any theological doubts or concerns.

GLOSSARY

Amidah	The central prayer of Jewish worship, introduced by the Rabbis as a temporary (they hoped) substitute for animal sacrifice in the Temple
Bimah	The rostrum in a synagogue from which the service is led.
Eruv	A legal fiction: a temporary 'boundary' that permits the rules of the Sabbath to be eased within its limits
Hebrew Bible	39 biblical books made up of the Torah (the first 5 books), the Prophets (including the 'historical' books, the 3 major and 12 minor prophets) and the Writings. These are in a slightly different order to the Christian Old Testament.
Israelite	A citizen of Ancient Israel – a description of the characters of the Hebrew Bible from Abraham until the destruction of the first Temple
Jerusalem	City captured by King David and selected as his capital city around the year 1000 B.C.E.
Jew	Taken from the term *yehudi* – description of the citizens of the province that became known as Judea in Greek and Roman times.
Kashrut	The Jewish dietary laws
M'zuzah	Small box containing 3 Hebrew paragraphs known as the *Sh'ma* attached to the doorposts of Jewish homes.
Midrash	Creative Rabbinic interpretations of biblical verses and stories
Mishnah	Collection of Rabbinic opinions and decisions compiled at the end of the 2nd century CE in Judea.
Rabbinic	Written by or pertaining to the Rabbis of Judea who effectively reshaped Judaism in the period of Greek and Roman rule
Sh'ma	(Deuteronomy 6:4-9; 11:13-21; Numbers 15:37-41)
Shabbat	The Jewish day of rest from sunset on Friday until sunset of Saturday.
Sukkot	The Jewish harvest festival that falls on the full moon of the seventh month of the Hebrew calendar, exactly six lunar months after the festival of Passover.
T'fillin	Small boxes containing the *Sh'ma* worn with the assistance of straps by Orthodox Jews at weekday morning services
Talmud	The combination of the words of the *Mishnah* and opinions stated about it by the rabbis who followed those whose opinions it contained, mainly in Babylon, (this was known as the *Gemarra*) were combined to make the Talmud, which was concluded around the year 500 C.E.
Torah	The first 5 books of the Hebrew Bible
Yom Kippur	The Day of Atonement, five days before the harvest festival of *Sukkot.*

TIMELINE (very edited highlights!)

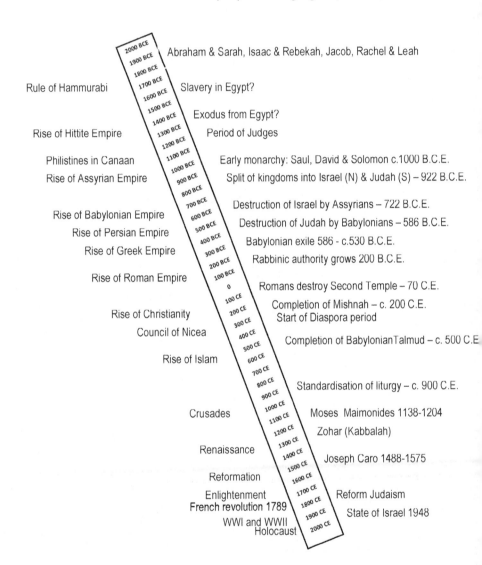

	2000 BCE — Abraham & Sarah, Isaac & Rebekah, Jacob, Rachel & Leah
	1900 BCE
	1800 BCE
Rule of Hammurabi	1700 BCE — Slavery in Egypt?
	1600 BCE
	1500 BCE
	1400 BCE — Exodus from Egypt?
Rise of Hittite Empire	1300 BCE — Period of Judges
	1200 BCE
Philistines in Canaan	1100 BCE — Early monarchy: Saul, David & Solomon c.1000 B.C.E.
Rise of Assyrian Empire	1000 BCE — Split of kingdoms into Israel (N) & Judah (S) – 922 B.C.E.
	900 BCE
	800 BCE
	700 BCE — Destruction of Israel by Assyrians – 722 B.C.E.
Rise of Babylonian Empire	600 BCE — Destruction of Judah by Babylonians – 586 B.C.E.
Rise of Persian Empire	500 BCE
Rise of Greek Empire	400 BCE — Babylonian exile 586 - c.530 B.C.E.
	300 BCE — Rabbinic authority grows 200 B.C.E.
	200 BCE
Rise of Roman Empire	100 BCE
	0 — Romans destroy Second Temple – 70 C.E.
	100 CE — Completion of Mishnah – c. 200 C.E.
Rise of Christianity	200 CE — Start of Diaspora period
Council of Nicea	300 CE
	400 CE — Completion of Babylonian Talmud – c. 500 C.E
	500 CE
Rise of Islam	600 CE
	700 CE
	800 CE — Standardisation of liturgy – c. 900 C.E.
	900 CE
Crusades	1000 CE — Moses Maimonides 1138-1204
	1100 CE — Zohar (Kabbalah)
	1200 CE
Renaissance	1300 CE
	1400 CE — Joseph Caro 1488-1575
Reformation	1500 CE
	1600 CE
Enlightenment	1700 CE — Reform Judaism
French revolution 1789	1800 CE — State of Israel 1948
WWI and WWII Holocaust	1900 CE
	2000 CE

BIBLIOGRAPHY

This list is not intended to be exhaustive; rather it offers some suggested further reading for anyone interested in Liberal Judaism and the Jewish view of God.

Dawkins, Richard: 'The God Delusion', London 2006

Fowler, James: 'Stages of Faith', New York 1981

Friedmann, Richard: 'Who Wrote the Bible?' San Francisco 1997

Goldberg David J. & Rayner John D.: 'The Jewish People, London 1987

Kessler, Edward (ed.):'A Reader of Early Liberal Judaism, London 2004

Kushner, Harold: 'To Life', New York 1993

Meyer, Michael: 'Response to Modernity, Oxford Univ. Press, 1988

Miller, J. Maxwell & Hayes, John H.: A History of Ancient Israel and Judah, Louisville 1986

Petuchowski, Jacob: 'Prayerbook Reform in Europe', New York 1968

Tobias, Pete: 'Liberal Judaism: A Judaism for the 21st Century', Liberal Judaism, 2007

Wilson, Ian: 'The Bible is History', London 1999

ACKNOWLEDGEMENTS

In addition to the members of the T.L.S.E. Tuesday morning adult education group, for whom this was originally written, thanks are also due to a number of other people.

In particular I am grateful to friends and colleagues who read this book at various stages of its creation, namely Rabbis Rachel Benjamin, Andrew Goldstein and Richard Jacobi as well as Beattie Sayers and Vivienne Schuster. Thanks also to members of The Liberal Synagogue Elstree and Temple Ner Ami in Camarillo, California on whom several chapters have been thrust in various guises.

To Watford Football Club, whose recent performances, especially from August to mid-December 2019, gave plenty of opportunity to contemplate various elements of this book while sitting at Vicarage Road. And finally to my grandson, Jaxon (b. May 2018), whose questing and questioning look, particularly in his early months, has inspired – and continues to inspire – me to search for meaning and purpose for my and his life.

PT, January 2020

Printed in Great Britain
by Amazon